EXPEDITION COSTA RICA

W. M. RAEBECK

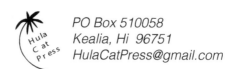

PO Box 510058
Kealia, Hi 96751
HulaCatPress@gmail.com

To Leonardo

~ *muchas gracias* ~

~ acknowledgements ~

With gratitude to Marcie Powers
for her unwavering enthusiasm, patience, and clarity in helping me
fine-tune this journal.

And heartfelt thanks to Terry Patterson for bringing me this adventure,
and for being my traveling soul sister through the decades.

~ November 1985

SOME THINGS YOU DON'T EVEN KNOW you're wishing. Some childhood dreams go wherever childhood went—the visions of ourselves on sailing ships, on isles of unnamed oceans, on expeditions crossing lands without maps. Different dreams come true instead, other islands are loved. And it's okay to never have chopped through the jungle with a machete or slept outside in the rain forest or known there were more days left on a journey than food to eat.

And when you're little, thinking about Huckleberry Finn, Swiss Family Robinson, Tarzan, and Balboa, you don't think about their feelings, just their determination, their distance, their guts, their guile. And you build forts, and everything happens fast. If it's exciting you jump up and down, and if it's awful you die quick. You don't reenact Christopher Columbus sitting in his cabin, head in hands, aching for Mrs. Columbus. You don't imagine loneliness or despair. And when there's mutiny on the bounty, it's the bad old captain's own stupid fault for being a mean, horrible person. You don't think that he might've been nice once but everything got too rough, that he never envisioned how difficult the quest would become.

And when we're older, maybe teenagers, maybe adults, we do think about the downside of adventure—the risks, the losses. And we choose safer journeys; we don't want to suffer. Besides, how do you get invited on an *arctic expedition*? How do you get chummy with Jacques Cousteau? How do you get on staff at *National Geographic*? And who's going to foot the bill? And how do you drop everything, grab your Swiss army knife, and head for parts unknown? You don't. You dream smaller and take more manageable journeys.

But you are what you are. You've still got your atlas at arm's length, open horizons still call. One way tickets are a gamble, but round trip is impossible...

My soul was stewing last spring. Having worked much too hard for a year and a half in the anti-nuclear movement, I was now wondering where to reinsert myself. I made a list of what still held interest at 35 years of age. It was short: travel, photography, nature, possibility. But soon, with a practical shrug, I said goodbye to philosophical indulgence, found two jobs, and camouflaged myself into the sixty-hour-a-week set. Both gigs were novel enough to temporarily hold my attention. Though out of place, I laughed a lot—mind over matter is a fine drug. I hid my list, and performed my jobs with a satisfaction akin to that of tossing a bottle into a garbage can from thirty feet off, "Wow, I can do it."

Four weeks into this behavior, I received a phone call that cancelled the solvent perspective and shot me straight back to the tree-house. I was invited on an expedition.

Suddenly all that spiritual tenacity and material skepticism were rewarded! It was okay to be someone who'd drop everything for a great adventure, someone with nothing to lose. Those are the kind of people required for expeditions.

The intent was to march into the Costa Rican rain forest from the east coast, locate a tribe, visit with them a day or two, then hike out the other side, emerging from the jungle on the Pacific coast. Orlando (my eccentric in-law) said the trek would take about eight days.

My employers could see by the light in my eyes that I was already on the plane, and agreed to hold my job for two weeks.

I would go, with the same abandon one might go to heaven. In five days I'd be on a flight from L.A. to San Jose, Costa Rica. A wish had been granted...or looked like it was about to be. A journey to take us outside our customary minds.

❧

In recounting this story, the names of places have been changed to protect the undisturbed nature and indigenous people. Today this expanse of land remains under strict governmental preservation, for the ecosystems and the people who call it home.

If you resonate with this tale, if you're moved by our experiences, let the book be your expedition, too. Hold the place sacred, knowing it's out there somewhere complete unto itself. It would be devastating for this book to negatively affect that region.

Thank you for understanding.

. . . . . .

This account was written as the experience was unfolding. I could never have remembered the details otherwise, nor recorded the emotional and physical highs and lows at some later date. When the journey was over, the book was done.

Since then, I've edited the manuscript numerous times — clarifying and streamlining things but never touching the story itself in even the smallest way.

. . . . . .

At the end of some passages are dates. These record the actual day that entry was written, often not the date of the action described. So don't be confused; I wanted to retain the journal as originally written, for the record.

~ W.M.R.

EXPEDITION COSTA RICA

PART I - IN GEAR

Moist clouds and light winds made San Jose balmy and clear, and a familial tranquility inhabited the townspeople's faces. With no falseness, no hard sell, they seemed refreshingly shy.

Perhaps the most courageous of our group, my sister Darcy had arrived first, with Maya and Marco, aged two and a half, and eight months. And, at Orlando's suggestion, the exhausted little trio even met me at the airport when I touched down from L.A. Orlando himself, Darcy's husband, arrived the following day and, here in his native land, was more relaxed than I'd ever seen him. Everything worked for him here, from friends and relatives to simple happiness at being home. In New York he was flamboyant and odd, here he was glorious and grand. And his care for a growing family added a practical dimension much welcomed by all who knew him. At dinner that night, I asked him how long he'd been preparing for this expedition. "Twenty years," he answered, with far-away eyes.

Orlando Nelson is a man of forty-nine who maintains a twenty-five-year-old's strength and physique. On the phone a few months earlier, Darcy had said, "Remember when I told you Orlando can run twenty miles on the beach? Well, make it twenty-seven." His outrageous generosity baffles people, and his extravagance throws mud at the notion of earning interest. Human interest, though, he's earned—from his Mayan excursion in Mexico to his art-related enterprises in Australia to his jungle treks in every Central American country.

The purpose of this one was to find a tribe reputedly living deep in the jungle of a region called Karakima, nearly ten thousand feet up into the mountains. What little information Orlando had gathered, from other tribes less remote, was that this one, the Locandias, had chosen to stay permanently apart from civilization. Anthropologically, there's surely a term

3

for seeking out an unknown people, but our motivations were lastly scholastic. Exhilaration, curiosity, and a yearning for closeness with nature and the Unknowable Great seemed the common incentive of the participants now gathering in San Jose.

After Orlando, came Brett, Stacy, and "Mr. Garcia," all burned out from preparations and delays in New York. Brett, big and blond, was Orlando's trainer from the New York gym. Raised in the Missouri woods, and part Comanche, he looked physically suited for the outing. Stacy, Brett's girlfriend, a strapping Midwestern farmer's daughter, made an equally sturdy first impression. A jewelry designer, she'd left a whole season of orders in New York to make this trip. Tomas Garcia, a staff photographer from *Time Magazine*, so impressed Orlando that he dared not even call Tomas by his first name. Originally from South America, Tomas brought to the group the welcome reserve of a non-American.

Because Darcy couldn't possibly make the journey with two tots, Orlando had invited me—to "witness it for her" and share it with her when (if) we returned. Over the phone, he had said sincerely that it wasn't easy finding the right women for this mission. When it was down to the wire, despite our acknowledged personality differences, he decided I was a viable candidate. I was reassured that someone who knew me so superficially had still seen my stuff underneath. Orlando's instinct crackled around him like electricity, and he adhered to it like law. So I resolved to tone down my own electrics on this trek and follow his lead.

Stacy and I would each have balked at being the only woman. And naturally we had both immediately asked Orlando if other females were being enlisted. Slightly ahead of the truth, as he could sometimes be, he'd told each of us that the other was, at that moment, packing.

~ May 7, 1985, San Jose, Costa Rica

BUT WHAT HAD BECOME OF ALL THE CARGO shipped from New York? After waiting three days in San Jose, the fourth morning we barreled out to the airport in full force. Tall, proud, and annoyed, we marched from cargo terminal to office to warehouse and around again for the next eight hours. Five hundred bucks later, those troubles behind us, we loaded the gear into Orlando's Jeep and a rented van, then checked out of our hotel.

That night, numbering nine (including Orlando's brother, who was helping by driving the van), we headed for Costa Rica's east coast under starry skies.

The drive was about a hundred miles. Halfway there, we rolled to a stop in front of a blue painted rooming house in the town of Turrialba. Orlando hopped out and disappeared inside. Moments later, he reappeared on the porch with a kind-faced black gentleman in a suit and hat. We took turns shaking the old hand and looking into the weathered face of Orlando's father. Darcy, meanwhile, tried to tally up for him how many grandchildren he had, coming up with forty—ten more than his own count. As our Jeep soon pulled back out to the main road, behind the rented van, Orlando told Darcy and I that his father earns money by selling peanuts in the park each day, and had been counting out the day's profits ($2.00) when Orlando walked in. This was the second time Orlando had seen his father in twenty years; the first had been two months earlier.

We reached the east coast exhausted, then turned in the direction of Orlando's hometown, farther along the silent road. The tropics inhaled us as we caravaned down the dark, desolate, palm-lined lane.

Punta del Sol had one no-star hotel, one bar, one store, and a post office. The roads were unpaved and few, cars fewer. Caribbean blacks, a few foreigners, and a potpourri of mixed children lived in small wooden houses on stilts. The paint was faded, windows stayed open, porches were gathering places in the rain. Both English and Spanish were known by all. Fishing was a big thing, the fish were bigger things, tourism was a little thing. And the folks were friendly but not the first to smile.

Orlando had rented two little houses for all of us. And, at the decision of the rooster next door, we woke to a shimmering dawn behind a green-gold screen of coconut palms.

As PROMISED, ORLANDO ROUSED EVERYONE at six a.m. to begin our physical training. After little sleep in San Jose and less in Punta del Sol, and knowing fatigue as my proven adversary, I rolled over for another forty winks, as I'd promised. But crossing Orlando, especially so early in the game, was like thumbing my nose at the whole expedition. The others dutifully attended his boot camp.

But when they all dragged in from their five-mile run, half on sand, then slept all day, I felt excellent being rested instead. Tomas had damaged a knee and could no longer run at all, and Stacy had twisted an ankle. (Stacy and Brett were also suffering the side effects of malaria pills, in addition to five other precautionary shots they'd each had in New York.)

The second morning at six, we ran three and a half miles along a jungly trail by the beach. A twenty-two-year-old native from Punta del Sol, Ernesto, had now joined the team—Spanish speaking and lithe and agile as a dancer. He had the face of a Lancelot, and his mere presence pleased everyone. He was the first of the young men we'd recruit to help with cargo. (When Orlando had done the twenty-seven-mile run two months earlier, along that road we'd just traveled, Ernesto had accompanied him on a bicycle.)

Running on the trail now, I was winded and floundering a half mile behind the pack, slower than even "Mr. Garcia," who was walking! When I finally caught up to where the others were running in place by a lagoon, Orlando pushed us into a series of aerobic strength exercises, all lost on me in a blur of heavy panting.

The third morning—after the men took a three-hour hunting trip in the middle of the night—we didn't commence our workout till a tardy seven o'clock. We ran only two miles, then for the next two hours did body-building on a wooden rack Orlando had constructed by the houses.

Being driven like an ensign was counter to my yoga-based notions of fitness training. Brett, our trainer, had allegedly been lifting weights for twenty-four years—impressive considering he was twenty-six. Soul-mate Stacy was no cream-puff either, and half their conversations were in some gym lingo I couldn't decipher. And Orlando could knock off twenty or thirty miles in a morning, and generally took life at a gallop—leaving only "Mr. Garcia," i.e. Tomas, as my possible equal. But he was a man; relegating me the uncontested runt of the litter.

I enjoyed this distinction so little that I decided to punish myself no further. Despite the once-in-a-lifetime opportunity before us, I felt my safety at stake under this 'training.' Plus I was alienated for being openly contrary. Without an ally it seemed dicey to venture into the unknown...

So I detached from the group. I'd continue the training, but not to over-exertion. I had to be true to myself, and would even throw in the towel if too compromised.

. . . . . .

The days blended together in a series of pre-expedition emotions and sore muscles. Our core group of five (Orlando, Tomas, Brett, Stacy, and I) spent the week as a unit, and though our differences became clearer, mutual excitement bound us. There were exhilarating periods of fearlessness, joy, and trust—but, simultaneously, for me, stubborn withdrawn times after clashing with the macho drive of Orlando and Brett. Nature had always been fair with me, and I knew machismo wouldn't fool the weather or the mountains. Reliant for so long on my own instincts, it was tough taking commands now. Orlando was our leader, yet I wondered where he'd lead us when I saw all the rifles and ammo, Brett's bullwhip, bow, and arrows.

EXPEDITION COSTA RICA

Were we going exploring or hunting? Both, said Orlando and Brett.

Before leaving New York though, Brett, Stacy, and Tomas had made a commitment to follow Orlando through thick and thin. Now those three told me, in unison, that it was imperative I do the same.

"Look," I responded to their serious faces around the table after dinner one night in Punta del Sol, "I've known Orlando for eight years. I wouldn't be here if I didn't feel I was up to the task...that's probably why he asked me to come. I'm going to do my best not to assert my independence, and simply do what's required of me out there— I'm going forward with that understanding—but I'm not going to swear that in any situation I'll do whatever Orlando says...or as you said, Brett, 'jump off a cliff if he says jump off a cliff.' I might—but with my life on deposit, I might not. If that really isn't enough, then you will go without me."

There was another week before they'd set out for the upper jungles of Karakima. We all continued enjoying the Caribbean waters, the glorious palm trees, scrumptious fruits, and tranquil sounds. Experiencing health again, after city life, is always a rebirth. And there was quiet time to meander, sleep, and mentally ruminate past and future.

Our training gradually became less intense...the reverse of what one would have expected. In fact, I'd learn later that Orlando's style was always to start out with all guns firing, then taper off. Now we were commencing at seven-thirty or eight. Mr. Garcia's leg began healing when he stopped running with us (and slyly confessed to me that he didn't like jogging anyway). And by the third morning, Orlando was humbled to the position of novice when it was unanimously decided that stretching was the best warm-up for our workouts. Presto, I was no longer the underdog.

Because our sessions were still heavy-duty, to ease the strain, Orlando furnished two masseurs who spent an entire Sunday with us under the palms, kneading our knots and soothing our pains.

Beyond Orlando's courage, determination, and vision, he not only made things happen, but with panache. After the harsh beginning, the amount of real torture each day had now lessened to about an hour. The rest of the time was filled with gratitude, feasting, learning, discussing, relaxing, and preparing for the unknown. In light of this splendor, my decision not to continue was scrapped.

I began to appreciate Orlando's uniqueness, too. How many individuals would single-handedly organize an expedition? How many would pay fifty thousand dollars bringing it to fruition? Orlando was the only one I'd ever met.

On the last day, we went into the jungle outside Punta del Sol for a taste of what was ahead. Like an ad in a camping catalogue, we set forth in the Jeep—everyone in clean clothes, bright bandanas peeking from pockets, fancy flashlights, and two-foot machetes slung from our belts. Only Orlando looked slightly scuffed, having been in the jungle every day. We numbered eight now, with Ernesto and two other local men.

Five hours later, we emerged from the jungle a different bunch. The trek wasn't unlike our expectations, just more extreme in every way. The ardor of upward climbing in dense jungle undergrowth, all at marathon pace behind Orlando, was balanced by the sheer glory of just being there. Going through a jungle is much different than going into one for a peek. Information flies at you: the juice of THIS plant can pop your eye out, the thorns in THIS one are nearly invisible, THIS fruit is eaten like THIS, the milk from the bark of THIS tree will make warts fall off, THESE little vines can be sucked on if you're bitten by THIS snake. Danger was at the constant center, encompassed by a desire to get through it with grace. Our clothes became liquid from the heat; the bandanas, around our heads now, were soaked.

The mountains here were actually more like slices of mountains, so sharp were their drops and so narrow their tops. You could slip with ease—on a log, a vine, a moist patch of leaves, a hole, some mud, or just the angle itself—and fall down either side fifty, sixty, a hundred feet. And that's just what Brett did.

Following the sound of a Tepisquinte, a small commonly-hunted mammal in these parts, Brett and Orlando were apart from the group. Brett missed a step and went down. Though he looked a little tarnished when they rejoined us, he was unhurt. Ernesto, on the other hand, was in his element, intimate with every plant and sound, communicating his knowledge with just a word or glance.

As we found our way back out, we were relaxed and happy. Walking five miles down the dirt road to the Jeep was nothing. Like the first football game of the season, we'd won, and the mud and sweat were souvenirs of how good it had been. Brett was quiet though, and fell behind with Stacy as we all moved along the road.

~ May 8, 1985

SETTING OUT

THE NEXT DAY, WITH NEW DEGREES OF SOBRIETY, Brett declared a rest day, rather than leaving Punta del Sol as planned. And, to our surprise, the rest of us actually regretted not working out. But the following morning, after securing Carmela as cook for the trip, we set out for Truluka. Bilingual Carmela hid her uncertainty about this unorthodox enterprise, appreciating the wages and reckoning we couldn't *all* be nuts. Plus she'd known Orlando her whole life. With a flatbed truck trailing with the equipment, the Jeep now led the way. Brett, feeling generally rundown, needed another day of recuperation, so he and Stacy lingered in Punta del Sol with Darcy and the kids.

Darcy's faith in Orlando and the mission was as unwavering as his. She and the little ones would stay in Punta del Sol till he returned from Truluka with the car. Then she'd drive us all to the edge of the jungle. Later on, she'd meet us on the other side of the country, in Cielo Grande near the Pacific coast. God willing, we'd be re-entering civilization in about fifteen days.

For those of us driving inland now, the adventure was beginning. Hotter than ever, we crawled along the dirt roads, ruts under us like waves under a speedboat. The flatbed truck carried water, and ice to keep the water cool. Orlando and Mr. Waldo, his stepfather—a spry old goat who lived in Punta del Sol, cut and laid banana leaves on top to keep everything shaded.

Kiri-kiri, the county seat, was essentially a bus-stop. Coca-cola was abundant, but little else. We stopped in front of an aqua shanty flying a Costa Rican flag and bearing signs of officialdom, like "No packages may be left HERE."

Inside was our newest recruit, a lieutenant called Manuel Abilar Martinez. He'd add the formal touch to our brigade, a uniform. And a few more guns.

That evening, we congregated in the 'dining hall' in the village of Truluka, a grubby little truck stop whose population was divided equally between chickens, kittens, puppies, children, and truckers. All were on hand and constantly regrouping around the table as Carmela served up huge plates of rice, plantain, beans, and Tepisquinte. A parrot looked on from atop the cabinet.

Orlando's Costa Rican accent was finally at home. Here on the East Coast, a pigeon-style English was predominant because most of the people had originally come from the Caribbean, though all also spoke Spanish. "Tomorrow night we go see the *sukia* man," said Orlando. "Tonight we go make a map. We talk to an old man who knows."

Orlando, Tomas, and I then spent a sweet hour in the candlelit shop of Luis Jimanez and family. In his mid-sixties and part Indian, Señor Jimanez counseled with us about the rivers, the hills, the tiny villages, and the native tribes we were trying to find. On blank paper, we played a line and dot game that would hopefully be the basis for our map. Wanting so much to register each word, my Spanish advanced probably a semester in that hour.

"Is there someone else also to ask? Is there someone around here who really knows the area?" Orlando asked Jimanez.

"Yes," Jimanez answered, "Padre Renaldo Sanders in Bamari. He knows everything."

Another man, short and strong, was looking on, and with little prodding, Orlando was able to enlist him for our entourage. This selection process, I'd been noticing, was refined and instinctual. "If I make a mistake and pick the wrong person," Orlando said, "I'm the one who suffer later. If they ask too many questions, then I know it won't work.

If they just say, 'I'm ready,' then I'm sure." Thinking about Tomas, Brett, Stacy, Ernesto, Carmela, and myself, I knew that, when asked to join the group, joy and honor had been our immediate response. Not knowing what was ahead, and knowing that no one else knew either, intrigued rather than repelled us.

Leaving Señor Jimanez, and taking our sketchy new 'map' (that I would be guarding through flood and hell-fire), I suggested we go the next day to Bamari, an hour's walk from Truluka, and find Padre Renaldo Sanders. But Orlando had doubts about getting advice from a non-native. (The padre was a gringo.) Or maybe it was native pride— you don't ask a foreigner about your own country.

When we got back to our rooms at 'The Truluka Ritz,' as we dubbed these barracks that would make camping seem luxurious, I found a spider on the bed post that was three inches from toe to toe. Ernesto performed the old cup and post card trick for me and tossed it out the window. Then saying, "*Siempre dos* [always two]," he disappeared under the bed and emerged a moment later with a duplicate specimen.

The next day was market day on the river bank and the first boats would come down river at six. At dawn, Tomas knocked on my door, as planned. The amount of daylight indicated we'd both overslept. But, without Daylight Savings Time, these mornings deceived—it was only five-thirty and we could still get there before the fog lifted and the boats arrived from up-river. With our cameras, we scurried out.

Green plantain, snug in the long hollows of boats, popped out of the grey as the gondola-like vessels neared the bank in the misty river-scape. In the distance, far away where the Relibo River [*Rio* Relibo] begins, was the deeper green of the mountains. Up there was Karakima, our destination.

This riverside, this market with two grass huts as the only structures, was a kind of social border, as well. Up in the mountains lived the tribes, each more remote than the one before it. There were three settlements we'd now heard about, and we hoped to find them all. The map-drawing attempt the night before was at least a start.

Today Orlando identified the different factions exchanging goods, and suddenly the casual loading and unloading from boat to truck became a multi-leveled interaction, perhaps even the stirrings of a future town— a primitive trading post where different contingents converge, exchange, then leave the riverbank as silent and empty as before. With the river as throughway, the Indians send cacao, plantain, and bananas down from the mountains by boat. These natives are a shy and private people, intentionally secluding themselves from civilization. They only deal through a go-between who delivers their produce then secures other commodities to transport back up-river to them. On the riverbank, trucks assemble, filling up with Indians' crops as quickly as the boats are emptied. The truck-drivers represent the Spanish-blooded majority of Costa Ricans, and differ in appearance from both the Indians and the Jamaican blacks of Punta del Sol and the East Coast.

Here in Truluka, merchants provide clothing and other supplies to exchange with the Indians. Every fifteen days they travel to San Jose to secure dresses and shirts that will be taken up-river to the tribes. So in-between the trucks and mounds of plantain on the riverbank are racks of brightly-colored garments.

These last few days before departure were spent researching the area and its traditions. As a native, much was familiar to Orlando, and we gringos pressed him for details, stories, secrets about the jungle. But Orlando was busily rounding up helpers for the trek, and maintained his velocity despite the humidity. The next day, after fetching Brett, Stacy, Darcy, and the kids from Punta del Sol, we regrouped over a late lunch.

"*Sukia* man only works at night," said Mr. Waldo, Orlando's stepfather, who'd accompanied Orlando the previous day on a recon mission to the Sukia's house. "This one is very good; lots of people were waiting hours to see him."

It was an uphill hike, but more through woods than jungle. Told it would take one and a half hours on foot, we did it in forty minutes. "Like a pack of hot red ants," said Stacy, as we welcomed the sweat back after two days with no work-out.

"This is paradise," I called out to Orlando, marching along behind me, as we passed a wood and grass hut on stilts, isolated among low hills, with broad-leafed banana plants covered in fruit.

"This is just the caviar snack," Orlando smiled. "It's nothing compared to what's ahead." We trekked on up through dense foliage and across streams. Such a well-worn path would've made it easy if not for the pace. And Mr. Waldo, sixty-four and an obvious influence on Orlando, raced right along with us.

The surroundings grew more idyllic as we climbed. Soft rises of lilting hills made it mellow and inviting, the whole area giving one the sensation of being swung in a hammock. Then, just above a glen of white birches, were two large wooden elevated houses, both with dried palm leaves as thatched roofs. Between the supportive stilts, roved pigs, chickens, dogs, and goats.

This healer lived in the second house but worked in the first. We followed Orlando and Mr. Waldo up the 'staircase'—a smooth log on end, with carved notches for steps. Most of the large house was without walls, except for one inner room that had two. Twenty or more people, mostly middle-aged men and women with a smattering of kids, leaned or sat in wait of a session. Overnight cases and packs showed they'd come a long way and were prepared to wait. Orlando had made an appointment though (aided by a little cash, no doubt), so we were privileged to troop directly to the inner sanctum.

Vicente Ernandez Ernandez told us, with Orlando translating from Spanish, that he wasn't actually a 'sukia' but a 'doctoro corandero.' A sukia, said he, was more a witch doctor than healer, who might help cast a spell as instructed by a patient as readily as help the patient get well—using his 'magic' for evil or good.

Orlando's interest in this particular 'corandero' stemmed from Ernandez's past. At twelve years of age, he'd begun studying with his elders, generations of coranderos, and believed that their knowledge and the passing down of information, strength, and power, was the essence of his healing abilities. At seventeen, after five years of study, he began working. Now, at "sixty-four or sixty-five," he had carried out the wishes of his father, who died at eighty.

"What did your father say to you before he died?" asked Orlando.

"'I'm going to die and you're going to live on. Cure people. And help your family. I want you to help your brothers and sisters. Help them with honesty—don't fool them. Don't fool anybody. And don't drink!'"

Then Ernandez told us that some sukias accept rum from people, or even ask for it, and that he had never done that. He did accept payment though, ten or twenty dollars generally from a patient, and seemed to be doing well—inasmuch as his wife and children had another entire house to live in.

Ernandez said he got all his power from God—or 'Skaga Yakira' as He is known—and that he directs this power into the water he gives his patients as medicine. "Skaga Yakira is right here whenever I work," he said, and offered us a sample of the water he used. Tomas, Brett, and I each took a swallow, and I can only report that "the power of God" isn't very tasty.

Ernandez seemed a good man. A little exercise might've livened him up a bit, but his face was kind. His eyes seemed to be weakening but his mind was clear. His main dietary staple was plantain, he told us, and he also enjoyed *pinolio*, a non-alcoholic corn drink. He never smoked, nor drank coffee, tea, or alcohol.

"He seemed a little sad," I said to Orlando as we made our way back down the trail with flashlights.

"He laugh when he go to the bank," Orlando chuckled. "And he also got a house in Beverly Hills."

Back in the Truluka Ritz that night, Orlando and I met with another man who knew something of the surroundings. In gathering information, we seemed to be attracting conflicting opinions about everything from paths to tribes to mountains to distances. Because tremendous rivers and mountains separated regions of Karakima, a wrong turn on foot could cost us our whole mission. Basically, we had to find out which river to follow, and four came together at Truluka. We'd follow either Rio Enok or Rio Relibo, but it had to be decided soon…

The following day, Friday (making nearly two weeks of preparations), we began the countdown. All the new helpers arrived at six a.m.—nine young men plus the lieutenant, who everyone called "El Capitan," and who sported a pistol tucked into his trousers. Brett and Stacy, our equipment managers who were dreading the ordeal, laid out each individual article of cargo, recorded it, determined into which pack it would go and who it would be carried by. As any onlooker would've surmised, this could be the beginning of a plaguing hindrance to the entire expedition—TOO MUCH STUFF. Darcy and I rolled our eyes, then took Maya and Marco down to the river—after futilely suggesting the sacrifice of such treasures as the chain saw, Brett's guitar, and a classic prop that even later, in the jungle, was somehow kept secret from Orlando: a toilet seat on aluminum legs.

As the day wore on, Orlando, Tomas, and I finally escaped briefly to visit Edmond Schlatz, a missionary from Indiana, who was translating the Bible into the local language of Kiri-kiri—no small undertaking—"so the natives can receive the word of God." A proud Christian, he was certain about his work and felt that the witch doctors here, or '*awah*' [the Kiri-kiri word for 'witch doctor'], used the power of 'Seeboo' (Kiri-kiri word for God) inconsistently and unwisely. The Bible, he felt, would sort things out.

Later, this same Schlatz appeared among the stacks of rice and sleeping bags at the Truluka Ritz and pulled Orlando aside "to clarify a few things." Having told us earlier about a boat trip he had taken up-river, where a military officer had also been aboard, he now wanted to scrub it from the records so there could be no chance of he, Schlatz, being mistaken for a CIA agent. (Americans here were all a bit paranoid in light of the Central American conflicts.) He now spent a good hour reiterating this—mostly to Tomas, who he knew was from *Time Magazine*—and being a general pest under a hot sun. What he didn't know was that Tomas was a photographer for *Time*, not a writer.

"CIA," Orlando laughed later at the lunch table. "Who care about this teeny little mosquito spy?" He slapped an invisible insect from his shoulder.

"I didn't like the way he was trying to talk religion at me," said Tomas.

"I know. That's selling," said Orlando. "That selling idea come from frustration."

Little mosquitos were welcome darlings, though, that night when Tomas walked over to a cluster of us with an insect the size of a kitten clinging to a stick. Gripping Ernesto in horror, I was informed by Carmela that I'd soon be seeing lots of these as well as cockroaches a foot long. By this time, Ernesto was stroking this Volkswagen beetle and coaxing me to do the same. It had a big poker protruding from its snout and little hooks on its front paws, but Carmela, Ernesto, and even Tomas seemed to regard it as a friend.

Another mapping session ended the evening, but three new points of view didn't end the indecision. "There's still time to walk to Bamari to meet Padre Renaldo," I said to Orlando. "It's only an hour from here. Or we could go in the morning." I was repeating myself but really wanted an experienced opinion. Venturing into the unknown jungle with the wrong information was beyond unsettling…

"Ever hear of Padre Renaldo?" Orlando asked the men in the room. They all had. "What do you know of him? Is he someone who really knows the area?"

"Definitely."

"Is he a good man?"

"He's a great man," they said.

~ *May 17, 1985*

. . . . . .

Orlando is outrageous, lives in Airean overdrive and abhors being doubted or disagreed with. But he's true to himself—a commendable quality. As my brother-in-law, I'd had a few years' practice with his personality. Tomas, Brett, and Stacy, however, had been riding on a magic carpet with him until these last few days. He'd wined, dined, and astounded them with lavish generosity both in New York and during preparations in San Jose and Punta del Sol. Now Brett and Stacy, faced with the reality of getting this equipment mobilized, thought we needed another day or two before leaving. Our group had grown to twenty-one people and everybody needed everything. Tomas, who had a June first deadline (it was now May 18) was not only concerned about going to no-person's-land with only eleven days to spare, but thought Orlando's disregard for available and possibly good advice about direction and mapping was annoying and naive.

Over time, I'd seen that Orlando's wild ways curiously worked out for him. Moreover, he'd definitely softened and humbled in the years I'd known him. From someone who once looked like the manager of a rock band, he'd become simpler, straighter, and more refined. I could now trust him in a familial way, focusing on the outcome rather than the method. I knew his mind was clear, his heart in the right place, his skills and strength limitless. His faith was abundant, too—critical in a leader. For me, it felt curiously okay setting off into the unknown with twenty other people, all in the dark about our destination.

Before we left, Orlando, sitting on a stump, stopped me as I was passing. "About the Padre," he looked at me, knowing this had been on my mind, "I'm not going to meet with him. It's not necessary for this trip. We find natives that tell us things on our way…we do it like that. I'm a native and I want to find out everything through those peoples."

"He might have some good information," was my final attempt.

"What he have we don't need. We get our own things."

"Okay…" I moseyed off. Things would be alright, but it sure wasn't the scientific approach.

Tomas fumed upon hearing this, regarding it as flippant defiance of both common sense and safety. I hadn't seen Mr. Garcia so livid.

❧

DAY ONE

THE RAINY SEASON HAD BEGUN a few weeks earlier, meaning rain began every afternoon and lasted straight through the night. Because the expedition had been so riddled with unforeseen delays, in both New York and San Jose, the rains were upon us from Day One. But you can't simply postpone an expedition for six months, particularly if you're Orlando Nelson. We were going, rain or no rain.

So at long last, we sallied forth in a blue open-backed truck. Orlando followed in the Jeep, also loaded down. We drove through fields and even through streams until vehicle travel became impossible. Our outfitted group was then deposited under a giant tree and the vehicles headed back, along with Orlando who was taking the Jeep back to Darcy so she could collect us on the west coast. The west coast? Were we really crossing the entire country through the jungle? Without directions?

During Orlando's absence, Tomas and I sat in the shade on either side of a stream, he washing his clothes, me writing. Across the field two people came marching. The second was a young native man carrying a light backpack, clearly for the first. The first was a sure-footed man of about sixty-five, with a walking stick, a long white beard concealing a possibly Caucasian face, and smoking a pipe. He, too, carried a light backpack and wore a round silver jungle hat. Seeing them, I tried to scramble across the stony creek, but was barefoot and couldn't move fast enough. So I shouted across to Tomas, "Stop that guy!"

Nimbly, Tomas was able to get the man's attention just as I came puffing up behind. This man had an air of… something. So without standing on ceremony we posed the questions that were still unanswered: Where were the tribes? Could we cross from one river to the other? Was there an existing course through the mountains to Cielo

22

Grande near the west coast? How many days from one outpost to the next? But first I just had to ask if he was Padre
Renaldo Sanders.

And he was—exactly as I'd imagined him.

Some of his information differed from what we'd heard,
some concurred. He'd been living here thirty-six years,
though, and seemed wholly knowledgeable. Secretly I took
his word for law; and trusted that Orlando's good sense and
findings would lead us along a course similar to what the
Padre suggested—at least until we reached the last tribe,
near the top of the mountains. From there even Padre Renaldo said there were no existing trails. He told us about
four Europeans, three men and one woman, who'd recently
set out from Cielo Grande on the west coast, attempting to
get through the jungle from the other direction—our plan in
reverse. He didn't know how long it took them, but on the
last day the woman fell down a hill, broke bones, and was
killed.

Soberly, the Padre suggested we head north once we
got to the top of the jungle, and make our way out to Turrialba (where we'd visited Orlando's father en route to Punta
del Sol).

But Orlando's intention was to walk *through* those
mountains one way or another (like the Europeans had attempted), ultimately reaching Cielo Grande.

Tomas and I thanked the Padre and said yes, we'd say
hello to the tribes for him.

Orlando's reappearance was met by hot, hungry, bored
workers and a confrontation with Tomas who wanted him to
listen up to what the Padre had imparted. I sat back in the
distant shade, knowing that despite methods, religion, and
skin color, Orlando would—in a relaxed moment later—listen to what the Padre had said.

So Day One of the journey was, by high-adventure

standards, diluted. In addition to the awkwardness of setting out into the green mass of bird-song and bugs in a human herd, two-thirds of whom were total strangers, the cargo was clumsily dispersed among the twenty-one of us. Two horses bore some of the excess, but it was decided after an hour and a half of walking that we needed more men. Passing one last hut, Orlando consigned three more guys, bringing the roll-call to twenty-four. Each man, though, had his own individual agreement with Orlando regarding how many days at so much per day.

Finding a grassy, level area, we made camp early the first day. Time was needed to organize the cooking routine, establish a streamlined method of pitching our three small tents, cleaning off the day's sweat from clothing and bodies, replenishing the water supply, and most of all somehow making the unwieldy cargo more manageable. To no one's surprise that last task took three to four hours the next morning, with everyone either working or standing by trying to help.

(This cargo was not the personal effects of we five Westerners, though none of us had just the rock-bottom minimum. Tomas, for example, had three large waterproof cases of photographic equipment, each requiring a man to transport. He also had a shoulder bag of more photographic gear. Orlando had one huge backpack into which fit all his stuff, and that he himself would carry 95 percent of the time. It's impossible to determine what was actually Stacy's and Brett's since they controlled all the equipment, locked it with combination locks, and kept it in their tent at night. Though not overloaded in the clothing department, they were continually able to produce rarities like Q12 Crab-lice Disinfectant, frisbees, or Beginning Rock Climbing manuals even many days into the journey. My load equalled that of a fair-sized backpack, but I carried a

smaller one and my additional stuff supplemented existing loads of two other guys. The pack on my back contained camera, lenses, film, journal, extra paper, rain poncho, space blanket, any food I could get my hands on, water, flashlight, and an emergency kit, plus a set of dry clothes for sleeping. Initially I carried my sleeping bag, too, but eventually had to bury it inside my supplemental load to keep it dry. Brett had instructed us to bring what seemed the right amount of clothing. But I'd recommend less next time, simply because two filthy T-shirts are really no different than four. We also had to take along sweaters for the mountaintops. Some things that I'd never before travelled without, but didn't miss, were: a towel, deodorant, an address book, money, makeup, skin cream. I often used soap for shampoo or no soap at all when bathing—the water was so clean.)

❧

PART II - RIO RELIBO

DAY TWO

JUST NOTES. NOW THINGS ARE coming too quickly. Too intense. Too much to record. At times I lose my memory of the details in the flow of sensations. All I can remember about yesterday's walk (it's Day Three as I write), is that two Indian women of at least fifty years of age, wearing bright dresses, carried bags for us with the men. Orlando paid them extra because they were so exquisite and strong... STRONG is getting to be the buzzword around here. Around where? Where are we??

Day Two took us upward. We entered the jungle. "Okay, now we're really on the way," Orlando said. That day we'd gotten muddy, sweaty, and worked hard. We had about twenty-four people. The load was immense, all the men amazing. I want to describe the place—but the place is becoming so overwhelming and consuming that only details about the people seem describable. But what popped for me, for us all, was the river.

We found a place to camp, an open area that our guide Indian knew was there. He said the river, El Rio Relibo, was down below, not too far. It was only two-thirty, but we'd left Brett and Stacy behind at a rest stop with some of the load that became too much to bear. The plan now was for Orlando and a few men to go back empty-handed, get that extra cargo, and lead Stacy and Brett to the camp.

While they were gone, Ernesto, myself, and two others followed a rough footpath that took us down to the river. There are still trails we can find. I am compelled by Ernesto's face—his soft eyes, defined cheekbones, and smooth amber skin—and his easy way of knowing and sharing jungle language. The four of us went down—an easy, though slippery, climb. Orlando and I had agreed that if the river offered a better campsite we'd move down there for the water, otherwise we'd stay above where there was an uninhabited wood and grass hut.

As we rounded a muddy bend in the trail, we could suddenly hear the river. It sounded *mighty*. A few more steps through high wild banana trees and there it was, pounding through, an almost monotone brown-grey with wide stony, grey banks with intermittent sand. Flowing straight in both directions, there it was, its thundering power radically offsetting the green-black depths we'd emerged from. Camping would be impossible down here—or I should say 'difficult,' since everything we're doing could be labeled impossible now. Like writing in the dark as I am presently.

We sat by the water a while. Then I peeled off all but my shirt and undies and submerged myself, letting the cold water run through me. A great relief from the sweat-flood we're growing accustomed to, about six hours a day now.

It seemed a shame to camp so far from this water, and a drag, but so be it. We climbed back up the jungly hill. Instead of sleeping in the tent with my 'assigned' bunk mates, Orlando, Tomas, and Carmela, I decided to sleep in the raised grass hut on stilts with some of the boys. With bark for floors, palm leaves for its thatched roof, I was in love with the architecture and tried to memorize its construction. Elegant handcrafting had gone into it, and though old and wobbly, it was sound. The staircase from the earth to the hut again was a tree trunk leaning against the edge of the floor, with four carved notches as steps,

Before dinner, Carmela and I went back down to the river to clean ourselves and our clothes. Simply indulging in the torrent was delicious. Not another soul around.

Eventually Orlando showed up—having returned from collecting Stacy, Brett, and cargo—and disappeared into the rapids. When he surfaced, he said he'd just had a massage by holding onto a rock under the white water.

Moods were a bit intense that night. Brett conducted a quasi first-aid meeting in his tent that Orlando tried hard to sleep through. And Carmela, who can go into a black funk at the least prompting, now did that (somewhat justifiably since she was lured into this romp with a seriously minimized vision of what to expect: "six days in Truluka" she'd been told). I was feeling fine because the walk, the river, and Ernesto were all so beautiful. And Tomas was a good friend now.

Under the embroidery of dried leaves overhead, Ernesto and I silently drifted off to sleep, not close as friends yet both completely severed from our previous lives. A storm had hovered since we first saw the river and in the middle of the night it split open and rain poured down. As I'd assumed, 'form follows function' and not a drop came through that thatched roof. I wondered if the three tents were doing as well. Experiencing rain with a roof but no walls was luxury. And the night was warm, just right, and free of things that bite.

Can write no more. If I turn on my flashlight, here by the creek on this mossy stone, then flying things will come and land everywhere. But in the dark like this it's ridiculous.

~ May 20, 1985 — Big, clean stream, delicious water, glorious camp

Day Three began like the others. The point was to get off to a dawn start, so Orlando got up at four-thirty, while everyone else fought off his noisy preparations and loud "Good morning! Buenos dias!" to anything that didn't move. By five-thirty, though, the camp was humming. I said to Stacy, "The name of this movie is going to be 'Frenzy.'"

Each day presented new obstacles, usually relating to baggage, and Day Three took the prize. Heading out, we simply didn't have enough man-power for the equipment. Some guys had only signed on for two days and had now turned back.

El Cassike, meaning 'The Chief,' who was our Indian guide, said today's walk would be four hours. Nobody flinched at that; we'd expected always to do six or seven, and had done only two and three hours of actual stomping the previous two days. But today was seriously wet from the night's rain, and The Cassike gave Orlando the sense that we'd have some work ahead. Knowing it would be tough, plus we were overloaded—without the two horses who'd carried a hundred fifty pounds each before they turned back—something had to be done. Brett and Stacy insisted that everything we had, including the toilet seat, was indispensable. Others felt we should part with some of it. Orlando gave Brett the choice: Come with us now and leave some things behind (forever) or stay back with the stuff and when we get to camp we'll send six men back to pick you up. Brett chose to stay. With Stacy, of course.

No matter what had been envisioned in New York, or what had been expected or implied, we were in the jungle now. The past, the future, and most conversation had become irrelevant.

Orlando had wanted to take some white Westerners into the Costa Rican jungle. As a Costa Rican, he felt that if he went alone or with other natives, there was no story for the Western world; so we four were his guests. He often reiterated that to me. But coming from L.A., I'd missed the New York preparations. Now it appeared that Brett, Stacy, and Tomas had expected an easier time—certainly in relation to carrying loads. Probably when there's money, and plans are being laid, it seems reasonable that extra people will be hired to carry the backpacks as well as giant cooking pots and tents. But it's an altogether different fairy-tale when you're covered with mud and sweat, grabbing at roots and vines on a vertical jungle path. With all due respect to who's hired and who isn't, the language spoken now is strength. In dealing with the unknown, you cannot afford unfairness, ill feelings, or anything that may backfire later. Equality is no longer an ideal but part of survival. Varying degrees of strength, like size for example, can be taken into account, but weakness cannot. Strength is willingness, weakness is backing off. And it was impossible for the group dynamic and the group spirit to have some members killing themselves with excessive loads and others carrying far less than their physiques suggested possible.

Today we left in two groups: "*el groupo rapido*" (the fast group), and "*el groupo lento*" (the slow group). Knowing Orlando's a.m. habits now—full steam ahead—and that he'd obviously be in "*el groupo rapido*," I opted for "*lento*," expecting individualized pacing there. Those in the fast group had to make radical time because they'd be the ones to head back again for the rest of the cargo.

Since we were splitting up, Orlando now assigned to me Wilfredo, an eighteen-year-old darling, who'd stay with me at all times. I had put in a request for a dedicated companion, after finding myself completely alone on the trail quite a few times already. Though I enjoyed the solitude, I was still new to the jungle, and being alone seemed unwise.

Our first fifteen minutes today were intense uphill mud, sweat, and humidity. Our "*lento*" group numbered close to twenty and we all stopped atop the first *loma* (hill) to shift our loads a little, sensing what might be ahead, though we hoped for something easier.

It got harder.

The whole day was deep, deep green. We saw little sunlight—had we stopped, photographs would've been impossible, it was too dark for anything. We could see alright, but the way was deep and the trail vague. The hills were so steep, so high, so muddy. We slid often. We sweated waterfalls. We hadn't enough water to drink, but sucked on some limes we'd gathered from a tree at that first stop. I was timing the trek to see if the four-hour estimate would prove accurate. We'd left at 9 a.m., but wouldn't know if we were making good time till we arrived.

I'd never experienced such continuous emotional extremes—mental and physical roller-coasters. On upward climbs, under the weight and heat, I always began filling with doubts—one after another, they entered and swelled. How stupid we were to not each have canteens, how stupid I was to entrust my life to another person. Should I turn back? I could still probably find my way back to Truluka... How bad would it get? Did I have any real allies out here? Everyone else was doubled up under equal or worse strain—if it got worse, no one could possibly take any of my load. Did I have enough strength to keep up with these twenty young men? Could I survive alone if I had to or got lost? Was God shaking His head at this?

One guy, Sinon, fell sick at that first stop on the hill today. He'd had hollow eyes from the start, and now in the first fifteen minutes wanted to bow out. Obviously he should bring his load back down the hill and go back, at least to where Brett was waiting with the excess cargo. (Brett, by the way, was our doctor, too, having been a paramedic at home.) In Spanish, though, the party resolved that Sinon exchange loads with a man who was carrying less and then continue with us. I was uneasy about decisions and discussions happening in a language I didn't speak, and doubtful about pulling a sick helper along. It seemed cruel. And what about the days ahead? Our excessive loads and insufficient work force complicated things dramatically.

Arriving at the top of hills was phenomenal relief. The last few bursts often involved teamwork—waiting for someone, helping someone, or being waited for, or being helped. This teamwork, just someone looking over their shoulder for half a second as you climbed over a difficult log, had real meaning. Even more meaningful was when someone got to the top, unloaded their pack and ran back down to help someone else.

And the jungle…it was ecstasy. Just being there at all. Away from EVERYBODY. Far far away. Knowing exactly how far it was from the last town, Truluka—a three-day journey on foot. We saw no one ever and no sign of any-one. Despite all misgivings, the feelings of victory at the top of these hills was unsurpassed. Dismissing all doubt in order to accomplish the task at hand was a lesson in the power of positive thinking. We were benefitting daily from out-doing and overcoming ourselves. It was sport without competition or congratulation. You silently observed your-self, ever mindful that the only success would be that final step OUT of the jungle. This was the ultimate challenge. Meeting that challenge was constant inspiration.

The hours went by with *El Groupo Lento* eventually stretched out probably over a mile. We'd stop when nec-essary to gasp for breath but basically pushed on. We never came close to *El Groupo Rapido*. I heard Orlando's bone whistle twice. (He had an ancient piece of bone, rubbed smooth from handling—his lucky talisman—that he blew into for sound. And I had a shrill call I'd respond with to give our position and assure him all was well.) To locate each other from one hill or valley to the next, there was much whistling, hooting, shrieking, bird calling—any sound we could extract from our throats and at glorious volume. The jungle absorbs all but the keenest sound. In fact, you cannot even hear the voice of a person walking in front of you (though you can hear someone behind you).

Due to his photographic load and a bad knee, Tomas was moving slowly. Keeping him in mind, I still had to do my own best. New at this, we had to continue to build strength. Ernesto seemed the one to keep in sight. Though stronger than me, he wasn't much bigger, plus he had a greater load, so his pacing suited me. In his eyes I put my trust and felt somehow that he was looking out for me, though not in a way anyone could observe. But today Wilfredo was my greatest comfort. I didn't know him, but found both he and his brother, Gregorio (seventeen), impressive, nice boys. As the day went by, Wilfredo stayed true, carried a massive load, surpassed me in strength time and again, and most of all, stayed with me.

Though following someone is easier than being alone out here, the experience is less poignant. After the first two hours today, I became more attuned to the trail, and eventually went ahead by myself just to sample walking alone. Most of the time flying solo would be loony, but part of the journey today was manageable. Plus Ernesto and Gregorio had powered on ahead, so in both directions I had back-up. After a while though, I slowed down on an upward climb for Wilfredo to catch up. When we finished the ascent together, I insisted we take a break. We sucked on a lime and just laid on our backs in the muddy leaves for half an hour. Though we'd thought the others weren't far behind, no one came along. It was unusual and good to have no one around nor any human sound. Seems we were always huffing, puffing, and working out or stopping in large groups at streams or on hilltops—rarely could we indulge in the pure sounds of just the jungle.

The final hour of hiking, we came upon Gregorio and Ernesto, resting as we had, and from there we four stayed together.

Ernesto had recently teamed up with Gregorio, and the adorable pair was so happy together that I just looked on in admiration. Friendship is so important in a venture this consuming, and I was pleased they could share the ups and downs. I had Orlando, Tomas, and Carmela to speak with, but Ernesto had been more or less alone till now, the language barrier separating him from the USA contingent. (Though out on the trail, he and I occasionally wound up together and easily shared an unspoken reverence for the tranquility, beauty, and power of the jungle.)

I felt sublime in the company of these three guys, and wondered if the four of us shouldn't just cut some branches and build ourselves a happy home right there. The peak moment came when, parched, drenched, weary, and filthy, we found some of the vines they'd previously told me about. Ernesto cut one with a machete, and a hissing noise issued from it, followed by a flow of water. We held it over our throats and our thirst was quenched by a kind of mineral water. We cut many, poured it into our plastic cups and drank. From there the journey was joyous, and later Orlando and Ernesto both agreed that this vine-water has strengthening and uplifting properties.

At one-fifteen we heard hoots, whistles, and calls. We must be close to the *Rapidos*. It had been four hours and fifteen minutes. Animal sounds erupted from us as we heard a stream below and then Orlando's voice. Hooting and whistling back, we wanted to slide all the way down the last descent, but knew, especially at these moments, caution must prevail.

We four were the first of *El Groupo Lento* to arrive and just twenty minutes behind the *Rapidos*. Orlando was ebullient and offered the stream to us like champagne. Bliss. Paradise. Friendship. The gratitude of safe arrival. The cleanest water in the world, and immersion into it.

But before we even got our packs off, five men from the *Rapido* group were already unloaded and set to head back to Brett. Leaving us at one-thirty, they'd get back to Brett at five-thirty. Without daylight savings time or any light getting through the three-layer canopy anyway, it would be dark by then. They'd collect Stacy, Brett, and remaining cargo, then lug it back through the moonless night. I didn't think it possible, but off they marched.

Making camp, tents were pitched as well as makeshift dwellings of plastic tarps draped over stick configurations. In a few hours a tiny overnight village was built—three tents and three homemade structures—everyone using all available space up and down the stream, but leaving slight wooded areas in between for privacy.

Meanwhile, as night fell, there was general agreement that a tiger was in town. One of the guides had seen a footprint and judged the tiger to be four hundred pounds. I didn't know if this was jungle jive or not but didn't enjoy the few minutes I found myself alone with no flashlight.

It was a weird night for me anyway because I misunderstood something Carmela said at dinner and sort of slipped away in tears. Passing Ernesto beside the cozy dwelling he'd erected, I asked if he could lead me to my tent because I didn't have a flashlight—there was a stream and some mud ahead. Pleasantly he agreed, as was his response to anything asked of him, and lit the way with his light. As we walked, he asked me if I'd heard any tiger noises, which I hadn't, then told me he definitely had.

"Really?!"

"Yes," he said, then turned back to look at me. Seeing my tears, he was sorry he'd mentioned the bad scary tiger. His apologetic look made me laugh though, as I assured him I wasn't crying about the tiger.

When everyone had eaten and retired, Orlando sat alert beside our tent, talking to Tomas about God while intently listening for the arrival of Brett's party. "If they get here by eighty-thirty, Orlando," I called out of the tent, "I'll eat the tent. And the tiger." I figured they'd show up next morning.

"They don't have any food at the other camp, though," said Tomas.

"Oh, dear. What time is it?" I asked.

"Eight-thirty," said Tomas.

"Hope you have a big appetite," said Orlando.

At eight-forty-five we heard their first yelps of arrival, and their final descent was vociferously encouraged from everyone below. And although Stacy gave me a good description of their unlit passage, I still had difficulty fathoming it—especially that the original five guys had made the trek three times in a row, twice with sixty-pound loads and once by flashlight.

❧

DAY FOUR

DAY FOUR WAS BUG DAY. I woke up on the wrong side of my sleeping bag. Orlando's four-thirty wake-up ritual was getting annoying. Tomas, Carmela, and I tried to out-sleep the noise, but the day had Officially Begun. We didn't set off till eleven either, and by then the energy was already on the wane. (Don Pedro, a local Indian man who seemed to live somewhere within a ten-mile radius, appeared at breakfast with his wife and daughter and they came along with us. They had also helped the *Rapido* group on Day Three.)

The turf today was to be similar to yesterday's, but five hours rather than four. This morning Orlando was steaming, due to frustration with all the cargo-related delays. And my tiredness clashed with his. "Stay with me, okay?" I asked Wilfredo, figuring I might need his help somewhere. And his eyes said yes.

With fatigue jinxing me from the onset, I was soon bitten by an inch-long ant. At the top of the first hill, Ernesto told me what to expect from the ant bite. The pain would go slowly up my leg, he said, and in an hour or so I'd feel pain in a pelvic gland. The pain would last up to three hours. And if, right when it happened, I had pee'd on the sting, I could've counter-acted the effect, but now it was too late for that. So I rubbed a little alcohol on it instead. And as the hours passed,   his predictions came to pass.

And not much later, I had a run-in with Orlando…over the issue of orange paint. Brett had supplied the original five of us each with a can of florescent orange spray paint to mark leaves or trees in an emergency, or to guide those farther back on a trail, at a fork, or difficult area. I found this paint noxious, cumbersome to carry, and less than ecological. Orlando made no comment but hadn't used his—just obediently transported it. These were our first days out, and getting lost was probably the most popular fear. In fact, we five kept our emergency first aid kits—space blankets, waterproof matches and even peanuts—dutifully strapped to our waists.

The spray paint was to keep anyone from going astray; it even glowed in the dark. And I would hate to lose Brett and Stacy even more than I hated the paint. So, recently, with Brett usually in the rear or coming in a second group and sometimes at night, I'd begun marking confusing junctions for him. Coming upon a section of trail or non-trail where one couldn't determine AT ALL which way to go, I'd spray a little paint for Brett's group. He and Stacy, inevitably at the end of the line, always thanked me for the orange dots or arrows they found on trees, maybe three or four times in a day.

Today for the first time, Orlando began fervently spraying an extremely long line on the ground to indicate for Brett which fork to take. Tomas and I, having now come to regard the paint as a tool, reacted simultaneously, "Orlando, don't use so much paint, we'll run out."

But perhaps the most dangerous thing one could do in this jungle was to give Orlando instructions. He shouted at me for a full five minutes, "You NEVER tell me what to do! This is not your business!! I KNOW what I do..." I thought he was going to charge me like a ram. The rest of the group stood in a wide-eyed circle.

My eyes were sweating more than usual now and I was too angry to walk another step. I contemplated a sharp right-hand pivot into the thicket, and muttered that if it was drama he wanted, well that just happened to be my specialty. The group now moved somewhat sheepishly off down the 'trail' (that even after four days in the jungle was not distinguishable to gringos).

Orlando's unkindness was uncalled for and difficult to abide. I walked into the undergrowth to pee, then just lingered there hesitantly, knowing the group had left. I no longer felt like following. I looked around for a way out, some other path or direction...to get away, to get OUT of the jungle. But guerrilla plants encased me on all sides, including up and down—direction meant nothing out here. Even sound was swallowed whole. Four days into the jungle now, there was no way I could find my way back up and down those muddy mountains we'd climbed. Except for rare patches, we hadn't even seen the sky since the second day... I had no choice but to follow the group.

As I emerged from the undergrowth, there was Wilfredo sitting quietly on his pack. Though everyone else had gone on, he'd waited. *These* were the moments when you needed help in the jungle, I was learning, not for fending off tigers and snakes. It wasn't even words that made a difference, just the smallest sign of loyalty or support. No one wanted to oppose Orlando, even when he was off the wall, because trouble had to be kept to a minimum (bad things can be blown out of all proportion under survival conditions); so there could be no taking of sides. Plus all these boys were under hire by Orlando. But we put our hearts into our eyes and sent messages that way, or communicated sympathy by just staying near someone, handing them a cup of water at the next stream, helping them lift their pack back on after a rest.

Still sniffling a little, I thanked Willy, and we silently started walking. But following the altercation, I no longer responded to the hooting or whistle calls from up ahead and could feel Orlando's nervousness about my potential disappearance.

Arriving soon at the top of a muddy hill, I decided to try sliding down on my seat, thinking it might be safer. But I cut my arm on a branch.

At the bottom of that hill, that took twenty minutes to negotiate, we came upon Orlando and the others. He was as upset as I about our tiff, and attempted to finish it by yelling at me again. Fortunately Tomas had recently counselled me to try the silent response to Orlando's outbursts. Desperate for any solution, I took that advice and became a statue now as Orlando shouted in my face. I even closed my eyes.

This, of course, made Orlando livid! And just when it appeared he might actually pop, Tomas stepped in with the calm of a flute player. Inserting himself between Orlando and me, he took Orlando gently by both shoulders. "Relax, Orlando," he said easily, "you're getting upset." Orlando looked at him in disbelief. "Come on," Tomas said, and led him away from me. To the amazement of the entire assembly, the dispute was suddenly over, as Orlando and Tomas strolled away.

Only two hours into our five-hour walk today, Orlando now wanted to make camp. And he asked six men to go back and get Brett while he and three others (including Tomas) went on ahead to "Bajo Relibo," the next civilization post and hopefully the home of a tribe. Calmer now, he asked me if I wanted to come to Bajo Relibo or stay here at the camp. I asked for thirty seconds to think it over, and my inner voice instantly said STAY.

Thus, Orlando, Tomas, and a few men vanished into the green curtain in one direction, six other men trooped off in the opposite direction to go back for Brett, Stacy, and more heavy loads, while Ernesto, myself, and a few others stayed to clear the jungle for camp. Within a few minutes, I was bitten on the finger by another ant, a red one this time. Ernesto dug in his pack for a special ointment he carried in a tiny container and rubbed some into both my ant bites. Then later, after Elieser found three poisonous coral snakes in the camp and chopped their heads off, Ernesto pulled a wasp out of my ear.

> *~ May 21, 1985. Literally in the middle of nowhere —*
> *up on a hill in the wooded jungle*

. . . . . .

The flavor of the adventure changed on Day Four; confusion peaked in camp that afternoon and evening. Without Orlando around, our small group confessed unanimous doubt about our disorganization. The Big Adventure aspects dissolved into the realization that we lacked knowledge, communication, and trust in our leader. Orlando's unnecessary assault toward me, something I'd seen happen with Darcy numerous times, but something new to the others, put the confidence that everyone wanted to retain in him up for questioning. This level-headed bunch now discussed what had happened so far and what might/could happen next. Maybe 'expeditions' inevitably have moments of embarrassment about group naiveté, but there was no one around to tell us that. Instead Carmela, Ernesto, and I took a hard look at the disappearing rations, our unmapped, unknown whereabouts, and the museum of tropical insects seeping into every fold. We had no idea where we were or where we were heading. We felt like we'd been spun around in blindfolds. Like trying to function without instinct, that crucial sixth sense had been extracted.

Orlando, whose communication technique had always been at best primitive, was now telling us almost nothing. He'd given me the option of continuing ahead with his group this afternoon—and I might have learned more about his 'plan' by going along—but my luck was down today, and it would be foolish to risk an accident when I could rest instead. Plus the separation would benefit us both.

For the first time now, Brett and Stacy seemed sensible rather than paranoid for holding their ground when Orlando suggested they leave equipment and supplies behind. Perhaps Brett's methods for doctoring and camping were more elaborate and sterile than native ways, but Brett at least was here, responsible, and ready. If anything happened we didn't even have access to native methods. And native secrets were removed even further by the language barrier.

So Brett deserved credit where it was due; he'd taken on a big job and continued the best he could.

So far no one had spoken of turning back. Except me to Carmela. It would be lunacy, of course. But this expedition at times felt equally insane. Like six of us sitting around the fire that evening, yodeling into the jungle depths for arrival clues from either Brett's party or Orlando's. They would come, they would all come, tonight or tomorrow, and everything was okay, but…

After an hour of sound signaling and hearing return sounds growing increasingly closer, Brett's group arrived. It was nine-thirty. Three of our boys went out to meet them, led by the dynamic Elieser, who'd also gone to greet them the previous night. I was waiting by the 'door,' that happened to be atop a criminal mud-climb, when Brett's ten stumbled in.

First in was Gregorio. It was a cool, quiet night in the camp but when I put an arm around him and looked in his beautiful face, the surrealism of it all struck again. He was soaking wet, totally winded. His load dropped from his shoulders and he said just two words, in English, "Heavy load." The others clumped in, all wild-eyed and drenched. Worse than the night before, they all had double loads this time—thanks to poor or no planning—and there was a wartime aspect to it, a fight to just make it. One thing, though, overrode everything: these people were exceptional. Everyone shared everything now. Everyone did everything. And there was much laughter and smiling.

❧

DAY FIVE WAS A WELL-PLACED HOLIDAY. I woke up between Carmela and Ernesto in a tent. I'd somewhat wickedly summoned Ernesto from his friends in Tent Three, saying that Carmela and I needed a man to protect us.

Orlando and Tomas' group was expected back by eleven this morning. Our thriving little village of about fifteen souls, meanwhile, got on with the day's work—bringing up water from the creek, cooking food, eating, cleaning up. Laundry had become an annoyance for all, and upon arrival anywhere we'd immediately tie vines together to serve as clotheslines strung between trees. By Day Five, dry clothes no longer existed, because with almost no sun getting through, the washed clothes stayed wet. Next day they'd be worn wet or carried wet to the next camp and rehung. About that time it would rain. So we each had collections of sweaty muddy wet clothes and 'clean' musty wet clothes, all foul.

Waiting for Orlando that morning, we packed up in prep for the five-hour hike to where there really was a tribe. Without him, we were simply a relaxed hive of directionless little bees—the a.m. FRENZY appreciably absent.

~ May 22, 1985 — Still in deep jungle hilltop camp

. . . . . .

But Orlando didn't come back at eleven. Nor at twelve. Different contingents ruminated the possibility that he might be gone another day, or worse. We called the group together, from the three tents and two makeshift shelters. With Carmela as translator, we pooled whatever tidbits of info

Orlando had imparted when last seen the day before. What we gleaned from the session was that no one knew exactly where he'd gone, no one knew where we were—standing in a circle of fifteen in the heart of the Karakima Jungle—and no one knew the way out...other than going back the way we'd come, as risky at this point as going any other direction.

Most of us didn't bother worrying about Orlando. Lateness was excusable in these parts, and though eccentric, he had his unique brand of caution. We agreed to stay and wait for him till the next morning. If he didn't come by then, we'd send some men in the direction he'd gone to try to locate him.

At one o'clock, though, in strolled Orlando with one of the guides he'd left with and three Indian strangers to help with the next leg. (Tomas had stayed ahead at the next camp.) With our excessive load, most of Orlando's daily energy had to go to somehow procuring more men—no small task in these parts. Happy to see Orlando, we all gathered 'round. He was definitely our chief. Fortunately for me, he told his story first in English. Fortunately for him, he apologized to me (not with 'I'm sorry' but with renewed warmth).

It's easy and common to question a leader, and to lose faith. But leadership is essential to success and to completion of bold undertakings. There were bound to be more doubts ahead...but I decided that the burning desire to be part of this quest had to outweigh misgivings.

Orlando's news today was that there was one family five hours from here, and that the fruit feast we'd all been anticipating would not take place there. "They have bananas," he told us, "but they don't share them. They don't even share their water and they don't look at you." He then said he'd managed to buy a pig, so we would have some meat, but warned us to expect nothing else, to be generous with what we had, and to politely wait for them to warm up, and he felt they would. "Most of all," he made it clear, "do not cut bananas. Only eat them if they're offered, and be very polite."

Orlando was, of course, prepared to purchase anything they'd sell, but he'd already discovered that these people—part of the Locandia tribe inhabiting the whole region (two hundred people dispersed over fifty thousand acres)—didn't want money, thought it was acquired by 'dirty' means.

Maybe they'd trade something for sugar and salt, someone piped in.

"They like sugar and salt," Orlando replied, "but they don't have anything to trade." The bananas they would give us, when we became friends—no shortage of bananas—but that's all they had.

Orlando's party brought back with them a dead bird, a Toucan, shot in the chest. As I'd known I would, I was having tremendous difficulty with this aspect of the cuisine. Ever since I'd seen two chickens carried all day on Day One, alive and upside down hanging from the side of one of the horses, and later in a frying pan, I'd reverted to my vegetarian ways. Supposedly we "needed meat to survive," but vegetables and fruit were my answer. The Toucan was the most exquisite creature I'd ever seen—jet black with brilliant yellow neck, red collar, black head, and a beak that nations would war over. His little black eyes were half closed and I could see no reason on Earth to sacrifice this rarest treasure to fill one man's stomach or half-fill two when we had plenty of rice and beans. I was glad at least not to have witnessed his shooting. As Ernesto stroked the silky feathers, Elieser stood by ready to pluck it for Carmela.

Orlando was beat. He lay on the ground propped against food bags, and spoke to the others in Spanish.

He was thinner and not quite picking up his feet when he moved around, something he tried not to do. After only forty minutes with us, he and the guide left again for the next camp, five hours away, where Tomas was waiting. Ten hours round-trip through outrageous jungle, just to drop in, give us the scoop, and deliver some new guides. We would've left with him, as had been the plan, but we'd just begun food preparations and that kind of travel is fool-hardy on empty stomachs. (Orlando made sure everybody got two hot meals a day—usually rice, beans, spaghetti, and sometimes chicken or tuna). If we ate first tonight and then left, it would be dark for the last hour or two of hiking, and Orlando said there was steep climbing at the end and a river to cross. So it was agreed a dawn departure was preferable—though we'd have to do yet another double trip, because, again, there weren't enough men for the cargo.

So Orlando left, and our happy little community resumed the chores. Ernesto and I took on the major project of consolidating and sorting out the chaotic bags of supplies, redistributing the food and cooking equipment—a messy task made delightful by his cooperative ways. His tireless drive, doing whatever needed to be done from long before sun-up until everyone had collapsed at night, had by now been witnessed by all.

I treated Ernesto as a special friend. With sweetness in his eyes, he seemed to have "the answer," and nothing could rock his little boat. By the way he moved his hands and moved through the jungle, I could see he registered everything, but reacted only when necessary.

As we scrubbed dishes together, me getting soaked under the little waterfall, and he dry and not even barefoot on the stones downstream, he told me that he had a farm forty-five minutes inland from Punta del Sol.

"Your whole family?" I asked, having been told by Carmela that he lived at home.

"No, just me," he said.

"Just you?"

"Yes."

"Is it forty-five minutes walking?"

"Yes."

"Through the jungle, or is there a road?"

"Through the jungle."

"Do you have a house?"

"No. I have to build one. But first I'm clearing a field for my cows."

"How many cows do you have?"

"Four."

"Where are they right now, while you're gone?"

"In Punta del Sol."

I was silent, and glanced at his face, then continued washing dishes.

At five-thirty the rains came pelting down. I was overjoyed because it forced everyone into tents and subsequent early sleep. In our tent, Carmela and Ernesto joked in Spanish for an hour or so as I admired their faces in the red glow of a camping flashlight, and thanked the lucky star that made me feel actually cozy in the middle of the rain forest in the rain.

❧

DAY SIX

IT RAINED ALL NIGHT, stopping just as we got up at 4:45 on Day Six. As was frequently the case, I was operating under wrong information, thinking we'd be traveling two and a half hours then camping again in uncleared jungle. At 7:30, with Brett and Stacy again staying back with equipment until ten men could go back for them, the rest of us set out. But as the morning progressed, I gradually became aware that we were doing the full five hours to the Indian family's settlement.

I didn't realize it at the time, but the Indians Orlando had brought back with him were this family—in fact, who else could they be? Now, Federico, an older man, and his son Rodrigo, were leading the way for us. At the same buffalo pace we had come to know. Like the other Locandia Indians we'd met, they were withdrawn and avoided all but the briefest possible eye contact. Today, though, having to lead us, both Federico and Rodrigo seemed to be opening up a little, even smiling.

~ *May 23, 1985 — Federico's banana-land near Rio Relibo*

. . . . . .

These hikes are advanced meditations, trials, workouts. Thoughts from remote corners of your life trickle in, between the rhythmic sound of breathing out and breathing in. Unlike city exercise, you're not thinking of body-beautiful. Fitness may be a side effect here, but the focus is strictly on accomplishing the feat. By Day Six, all questions about whether or not I was up to the task, whether it was too dangerous, whether we were all gonzo and done-for, had faded into a more lucid trekking method. Now I just followed the boots in front of me. Today they were Wilfredo's, who had promised again to stay nearby through thick and...thick. If Willy's feet crossed a stream on stepping stones, so did mine; if his climbed an eighty-nine degree hill, using gnarled roots as haphazard stairs, so did mine; if his feet moved like skis and careened zig-zag through the mud down an eighty-nine degree decline, so did my backside.

I actually quite enjoyed the downhill skiing element of getting there only by sheer abandon, because too much caution created worry, interrupting the flow of positive energy—critical ingredient out here. We all loved it. And group abandon was particularly exhilarating. And that's why, even though Tomas swore the expedition was in essence a comedy, I would stay to the end, whatever happened. The physical exertion, sense of collaborative achievement, and divine purity of the places were life experiences I already looked forward to looking back on. How could I hold a calendar or job over untouched jungle?

Orlando was one of those people who has his own non-translatable credibility. It wasn't until this trip that I ever understood why my sister had married him. Even in writing this log, I wonder if I can depict his uniqueness enough to show why twenty-four people would put their lives in his hands and follow him into a jungle with no clues to their whereabouts or destination, and...have a good time doing it. Theatrics certainly played a part, Orlando hardly boring or predictable. Happy endings figured in it, too—we felt covered somehow. And for all the potential suffering, so far none had been actual. (So far.) Also, when confronted about the purpose of the mission, or why we tore through the undergrowth with machetes when there were roads that went around these jungle and mountains, Orlando's answers, though perhaps only in the tribal context, were reasonable: "Out here, we want the native experience, not the white man's. We don't look for the easy way, we look for knowledge of the jungle, of the history, the spirit of these people…of the land, the rivers here." But Tomas found this amusing. Accustomed to the linear trajectory of assignments and deadlines, slogging through mud for no tangible reward was fuzzy for him. And he missed his girlfriend. But suspension of one's outside reality was requisite for this undertaking, and Tomas wasn't willing to entirely suspend his.

Maybe we were being romantic, trying to capture moments of pure human existence. But we'd found it. There were no roads or wheels, electricity or post offices, no forks or books. When we talked of routes from one place to another, even if there were three different ones, as seemed the case in getting from our last camp to this tiny settlement, they were all savage jungle footpaths.

However, from this family's dwelling up ahead, apparently it was only one full day's trek to some remote outpost from which one could actually catch a bus to civilization… Not a factoid to be breezily dismissed by any of us.

The hike on Day Six was sublime, though the last hour was rough and I can only say thank God for the river we finally got to, and the sound of it forty-five minutes in advance as incentive to continue. Dear Wilfredo let Gregorio, Ernesto, Federico, and Rodrigo all disappear from view as I stumbled slowly along the river rocks, wanting each desperately as a chair and eventually selecting one. Willy filled my cup twice with the sweetest water I'd ever tasted, then smiled and drank some too. We knew others were still falling down the mud mountain behind us and that, although we wouldn't photo-finish with the champs, we'd still make decent time.

The water helped, and the final effort was pleasant. My Swatch watch ("with all the guts showing," as Carmela described its innards on display) was verifying four and a half hours of nonstop work, so we couldn't have much farther to go. Then rounding a rocky bank, we saw not only the faster folks sitting in the shade, but Orlando and Tomas waiting there for us, clapping their hands and coaxing us over the final waterfall crossing. As we stepped to dry land, they handed each of us a banana.

It would be another twenty minutes to the farm, but that could wait. Dropping my packs, I ate the most scrumptious banana ever, then dissolved into the river to be massaged, Orlando style, by the waterfall—fully clothed since forty male eyes were now trained on my every move.

Federico's property (or Bajo Relibo as this 'town' was named), consisted of a large grass-roof hut housing Federico and his family, and two smaller huts—an empty one across their stream where our contingent was nestling in, and one adjacent to the big hut. We instantly pitched the one tent we'd brought. And the lieutenant, now known as "El Capitan" or just "Cappy," threw up his customary plastic rain shelter and hammock.

Here in Bajo Relibo, it turned out another visitor was residing in that third hut. Chela, a twenty-four-year-old woman from Ecuador was a student from Ohio University doing her thesis on the ecological balance between humans and nature here. I figured the balance was pretty damn good with four people for every six or seven mountains of teeming greenery. But for Tomas this added to the farce, "How remote could we be if there's a student here from Ohio University?"

Chela was as shocked to see us as we to see her. Relaxed and easy-going, she clued me in on logistical details—like north, south, east, and west—that Orlando found irrelevant. And she was the one who mentioned the "busstop," two days from here—up and down the mountains. She was automatically a friend.

With Brett and Stacy a day behind us, I was the only American in the entourage, the only non-Spanish speaker (though improving), one of only two women, and to my surprise, as I chanced upon a three-inch square broken mirror in our hut, the only blue-eyed person in the vicinity. "What on Earth are YOU doing with this group?" Chela needed to know (though her own presence here was equally far-fetched).

"Stand by for two more gringos," I told her, "and equipment enough for the film version of this." The toilet seat on legs, symbol of our excess, was still with us, and Brett had put it to use this morning mere inches from the campsite, in full view of the entire company!

After settling into the comforts of a domestic camp, and gratefully accepting three more bananas from various friends, I took a leisurely two-hour stroll back along the trail to the river—not for the exercise, believe me, but to find my lost walking stick, cut that morning by Elieser. Moments alone were rare and restorative, and walking slowly a joy. Reaching the river again, my nakedness didn't offend or entice the mountains, birds, water, air, or stones. So I lay in the pool of a sunny waterfall knowing no one was coming from any direction until this time tomorrow. The rivers were the only places now that offered open space, and with that came peace and awe. The motion and thunder of the river were overwhelming compared to that stillness inside the jungle. Life was just enormous all around, my humanness completely extraneous to it.

Bathing was probably the ultimate luxury of the trip. The sounds of the water, the cleanness, the green and stoney privacy of the shadowy pools along curving streams... You'd just take your soap, or not take your soap, and meander along. A deep cove or nice flat stone would engulf you and hours could pass as you floated, washed, washed clothes, drank water, and collected it to bring back to camp.

✧

WE WERE MOVING FAR TOO SLOWLY NOW. On Day Seven there was no movement at all.

At five, everyone was up as usual. But I stayed in the tent with Tomas mainly because we were in a grassy field, for once, that felt like a featherbed. At six, once Carmela had plied them with strong Costa Rican coffee, I saw Ernesto and three others march off down the trail at a good clip. The night before, Carmela had listed her cooking needs, and today these four would hike seven hours to Terra Verde, the closest thing to a town, buy what they could, then hike back. At dark they'd make camp, and finish the return trip tomorrow morning.

I asked Chela, the college student, if the walk to Terra Verde would, in fact, take seven hours. Second opinions were rare and helpful around here, and she'd arrived here from that direction two weeks earlier. "Well, the way people walk around here," she said, "it probably *could* be seven hours." Apparently Orlando didn't have a patent on the speed of light. And we definitely wouldn't be seeing those four guys again until Day Eight.

It was good to see Ernesto go because I was feeling a little awkward around him now. In this setting, every small gesture was registered by all, so he and I now seemed to be almost avoiding each other.

Human interaction under these circumstances was altogether different than back home. The only effective way to show your good intentions here was through offering. Trying to "be nice" by smiling for no reason was meaningless. That's why the natives looked away until they knew who you really were. And while avoiding your eyes to protect their privacy, they'd glue them back to you when you looked away— everybody watched everybody all the time, it was impossible not to, human interaction was the only show in town. Carmela and I, as the only females in a celibate male camp (Brett and Stacy were rarely with us and were regarded as one person anyway), were obvious focal points, and there was curiosity as to what, if anything, might develop.

Today I washed a mountain of moldy clothes with Carmela, cooked a plantain stew, went to Chela's hut (or *rancho*, as these dwellings are called by the Indians) and looked at her geographical map, and filled in my journal. That evening, Orlando, Federico (the father), and Rodrigo (the son) returned from fishing carrying an ancient stone urn they'd found, worth probably thousands in New York.

"Will you sell it in New York?" I asked Orlando.

He looked at me sharply. "Never. These things is precious. These things is from The Expedition. This is good luck. Not to sell such a thing."

Brett and Stacy's team, natives first, came trickling in just in time for the best fish we'd ever tasted.

Later, "El Capitan" cut his finger, a small cut, and asked me for a band-aid. As I was fetching one, Orlando told me to put some of Brett's magic medicine on it. Not wishing to administer medications that I wouldn't use myself, especially for so mild an injury, I suggested Orlando ask Tomas or Brett to do it—they were right there and didn't have the reservations I did about medicine in general. But Tomas told me later that Orlando read my reaction as defiant.

~ May 24, 1985 — Banana-land

❧

DAY EIGHT. STILL CAMPED AT FEDERICO'S. At a standstill till the boys returned from Terra Verde with more food. Due to all the return trips to collect Brett, Stacy, and the excess baggage, we were losing heaps of time. So the food wasn't lasting the distance it was expected to. Plus all the additional men meant far more consumption.

With a serious face, Orlando requested a word with me. I was wearying of trying to follow him and his commands—with no information as to where we were going, who our guides were, or whether there was any overall plan. But I accompanied him to a secluded bush to talk. We were so radically different that even our most innocent attempts at working together could clash. Now he wanted a promise that everything was going to be smooth sailing, that I would do whatever he said no matter what. I told him I really couldn't make that promise.

He had zero tolerance for this attitude and suggested one of the boys guide me to Terra Verde from whence I could jump a ride with a Standard Fruit Company truck back to civilization. I said I'd prefer to stay with the group until Alto Relibo, supposedly two days from here. (Alto Relibo, at the top of the Relibo River, was reputedly the home of most of the Locandia Tribe.) From there, I could hike out with Tomas, who'd now run out of time and planned to leave us there to get back to New York. With natives to guide him and carry his equipment, he'd travel two days to a village called San Felipe, then get a bus to Turrialba, a town in north-central Costa Rica, then finally another bus to San Jose.

"No," said Orlando, "Tomas do what he have to do. Your things is different." Orlando wasn't enthralled about my friendship with Tomas because he rightly surmised that some of our discourse may be about him. (In fact, Tomas had reminded me, right before this tête-a-tête, to stay cool at all cost.)

Orlando actually wanted me to stay; the talk of sending me out was a ploy. When calm, he frequently reaffirmed that the success of the expedition, in relation to the "Western World," hinged on the four gringos getting through it. And now Tomas was leaving. Plus there was growing doubt about whether Stacy and Brett could travel light enough or fast enough to continue with us. Gnarly rumors about Aguila Mountain up ahead had already wafted through the camp...

I told Orlando straight that I couldn't tolerate undue aggression or being shouted at in front of everybody and that an apology was in order. And after a song and dance about how I should be the one to apologize, he did say he was sorry. But he hadn't annulled the Terra Verde alternative—we'd surely get back to it later.

While Orlando and I were negotiating my fate, Brett—now known as "El Doctoro," thanks to his elaborate array of medical paraphernalia—had examined three natives and dispensed aspirin and pain killers to all. Brett's new credential gave Orlando just the advantage he needed to get closer to the shy Indians. Today's excursion would be to "Sley," a settlement an hour and a half from Federico's farm in Bajo Relibo. Tomas would take pictures while Orlando befriended and interviewed the two families there, and El Doctoro would take a look at a man who was seriously ill and in need of help.

As they trooped off, I stood on the hill and appreciated the first peaceful moment since our arrival here. Carmela, Wilfredo, and I were the only ones left—it was still too early for the guys to get back from Terra Verde. Standing there, I could see Chela sitting in her hut with her books, and called across the stream inviting her to come down to bathe in the river with Carmela and me.

As we three strolled through the jungle toward the river, Chela had a mouthful of news and wasted no time sharing it. She didn't have all the facts, she said, because much of what she'd heard was in the Locandia tongue, but the gist was that the natives were threatened by us. In fact they'd been having heated discussions about what to do about this *invasion*. Our unprecedented arrival, a militia from their perspective, could only mean trouble. The appearance of large groups of outsiders was the beginning of the end as far as they were concerned, and exactly what they'd always feared would happen to them. So they were weighing their options—the obvious one being not to assist us in any way. They knew that without guides we'd be crippled.

From the Indian viewpoint, the scenario was this: First Orlando appeared with Tomas and two native guides. The next night seven or eight more of us arrived—including two women (Carmela and me), one white—pitched a tent, cooked food, and used the stream to wash everything. The third day, ten more came, two more tents popped up, and as the morning passed, four different contingents set off into the jungle in four different directions, all with rifles and/ or machetes. Where were we going? Who and how many would we bring back? Who were these four white people? How would they get rid of us if we chose to just stay here? Chela said they even suspected that she was a part of our gang, sent in advance to spy on them. She hadn't been able to convince them otherwise. For this reason, to prove her loyalties, she would now have to keep her distance from us.

Chela also said that an Indian friend of Federico's, who'd been passing through from Sley, as well as the local Sukia who'd arrived to cure Federico's wife, had joined in the debate about who the heck we were and what the heck we wanted. Since no one from CONAIT (the Council of Indian Affairs, a ministry governing these preserved lands, organized to protect all the Indians here) had informed the Indians of our entourage, it meant we hadn't been cleared by those channels (channels that Orlando, of course, was happily unaware of). All the more reason to take us for invaders, or even Americans coming to farm marijuana. And Orlando's charm, cash, sincerity, and spiritual lingo, though fascinating and tempting, left them sorely uneasy. (I hated to tell Chela that Orlando had a similar effect on natives in New York.)

Chela went on to say that despite their misgivings, both Federico and Rodrigo would continue working for Orlando. The only other way they could earn money was by farming cacao and selling it in the teeny store in Terra Verde, the single marketplace in a twenty-mile radius. Orlando's offer of paid work plus a full-blown adventure, gringos included, had the same dramatic appeal to them it had to us: go for it!

"But up-river," Chela said, "in Alto Relibo, they've already heard about you, and they don't like the sound of it. They aren't going to help you at all."

At three-thirty that afternoon, Ernesto and Elieser emerged from the jungle across the stream, and ran down the last hill, laden with provisions from Terra Verde. They had the wild warlike look of exertion that we were getting used to. They said it took seven hours getting there yesterday, and coming back with cargo today had taken nine and a half. The other guys would be here soon, they said.

Meanwhile Orlando and Brett had returned from their mercy mission in Sley and Orlando was calling a gringo pow-wow to discuss "the situation" between himself and me. I sat quietly through it, shedding an unnoticed tear or two. This session lasted nearly two hours, with Orlando airing his feelings first, followed by Brett, then Stacy, then

Tomas. When my turn came, I told them all simply that whatever was best for the expedition I would be agreeable to, including leaving the group tomorrow. (What I didn't say was that Carmela had secretly told me that if I left, she'd leave. As the only women beside Stacy—who was inseparable from Brett and usually a day behind—we were friends and confidants, and both knew our difficulties would increase without the other.) Once again, Tomas was the diplomat, soothing the roughness a little and bringing emotions to light without hurting feelings. And the little pow-wow served to unify our original core group again because Orlando was shown that Brett, Stacy, and Tomas also had doubts and disagreement about his methods.

I knew Orlando had no interest in Chela's babblings. To stay on the safe side, though, I asked him later that night if he wanted to hear anything she'd told Carmela and me. His response was, "You can do whatever you want with what you hear. You can write it down, talk to the others, what you want. But I don't want nothing of this stuff. I don't listen to no one! I just stay like an animal in the jungle." I definitely did share Chela's commentary with Tomas, Stacy, and Brett because we gringos needed to tread extra lightly around here, plus I knew these three, like me, wanted all the information they could get.

~ May 26, 1985 — Still at Banana-land

DAY NINE

DAY NINE. TOO LONG AT FEDERICO'S. Happy to be heading out. Tomas and Orlando had spent four whole days here, the rest of us three. Now, with local help—including Federico, Rodrigo, and some Indians Orlando had won over and recruited from Sley—we were able to push off all together for once. But not till eleven. Getting up at four-thirty or five and not leaving till eleven seemed absurd, yet the sunny mornings were well spent washing and drying clothes and sorting our clumsy supply of kitchen equipment.

We worked out on Day Nine. A breathtaking march, but about six hours long. An hour into it, in the scorching mid-day sun, Brett suddenly collapsed by an artery of the river. Feebly claiming he had sunstroke, he instructed us to follow his paramedic advice, that he lucidly dispensed throughout the trauma. He believed he'd carried too heavy a load (not his usual featherweight pack). However, he'd also breakfasted on grease and starch—white-flour "fry cakes" and white rice, all cooked in lard—and had been sunbathing all morning, ignoring everyone's warnings that the late morning tropical sun isn't for tanning.

So we broke open packs of dry ice, massaged his hands and feet, and wrapped him in space blankets. His extremities, he said, were numb and he felt like someone was sitting on his chest. He seemed to be fearing for his life. Muttering faintly that a heart attack at a time like this was entirely possible, he continued to instruct Stacy, Ernesto, Orlando, and I with detached clarity. Massaging his feet, as a precious hour lapsed, I wondered why it was always Brett having the mishaps. Was it not perhaps another scene for Tomas's comic rendition? After Brett's episode, and subsequent miraculous, one hundred percent recovery, some of us concluded that he was illustrating the value of his mobile pharmacy, hang the time-loss and financial toll on Orlando.

We had been just nearing Sley when Brett gave out, so one of the Sley Indians with us had gone ahead and sent back a young boy of eleven to carry Brett's pack. Then we all marched on leaving Wilfredo with Brett and Stacy, as they trailed weakly behind. We'd reunite up the trail in Sley.

The overall downtrodden appearance of the natives in Sley detracted from their refined bone structure. They were standoffish, shy, and suspicious, and didn't smile much. But they'd sweetly return my smile when caught off guard. After Chela's soliloquy, I knew what they were thinking and, mostly with my eyes, did all I could to quell their fears. But we couldn't expect them to trust us, and didn't push our luck. We all remained quiet and Orlando merely asked to buy bananas and plantain (of which they had excess since it was their staple), and a chicken to take to our next camp. And they obliged.

Though I'd been prepared to eat meat "in order to survive"—as Brett and Orlando had lectured us back in Punta del Sol—I was repulsed by the killing of the animals and could touch none of the meat Carmela served. Instinctively reverting back to vegetarianism, I ate just fruit (sugar cane, banana, orange, plantain, lime), rice, and beans with onion and garlic. And I felt remarkably well. The others dined on white sugar in lime juice, spaghetti with meat cooked in lard, and doughy "fry cakes" for breakfast. I steered clear of all that, knowing my health would mean my strength. A cup of strong coffee before the hiking, though, proved a critical mood enhancer. And a good night's sleep (tricky in Orlando's tent since he preferred the flashlight on, prayed aloud for an hour at dawn, and urgently asked throughout the night, "What time is it?")

While waiting for Brett in Sley, Orlando was also able to purchase dozens of oranges, to be instantly gobbled like jelly beans. Several corn tamales, too, came into our possession, but disappeared so quickly they may have been imagined.

In a while, Brett, Stacy, and Wilfredo lumbered in. But as we suited up, lifting loads to shoulders, Brett looked displeased. After three days in the last camp and only one hour of hiking so far today, no one wanted to hang back for one person's questionable malady. Orlando, more practical than sympathetic, told Brett to either come with us now, at a slower pace if he wished (we'd mark the way for him with orange paint), or stay overnight with the Indians here and join us tomorrow. His choice. Either way, the eleven-year-old boy would be hired to carry his pack. With that, Orlando vanished into the jungle followed by the rest of us.

Brett and Stacy followed.

Rio Sussio, or Dirty River, was our next destination. But having sacrificed over an hour with Brett, then pausing in Sley would mean getting to that river after dark.

My own reservations had now shifted. I was totally cool walking alone through the jungle—especially here where we followed the river for several hours. Though we were far above the water and winding along a craggy cliff, the trail was visible, so getting lost was a non-issue. And I quite enjoyed lollygagging along, singing or thinking, and knowing that up ahead somewhere, who knew how far, Orlando was breaking the speed limit with "El Cassike" ("The Chief"), the Locandia Indian who'd been with us since Day Two, and back behind me were Carmela (frowning and moping and cursing her fate) and El Capitan. Cappy, always cheerful and utterly cooperative, now held up the rear no matter what the circumstances. Whenever the whole group stopped, for water or a rest, once we saw Cappy coming up the trail we knew everyone else had filed in. When we didn't see him— not infrequently, as he was a tad slow on the uphill—we anxiously waited.

Today everyone was confused about distance because we'd been told two and a half hours. But, unbeknownst to all but Orlando, about halfway along Federico had said, "Let's go all the way." Orlando had agreed, but they'd kept it their little secret.

Alone, I finally stumbled down the last cliff to Rio Sussio, reaching bottom just as darkness set in. Cappy and at least ten others were way behind me. Hopefully with flashlights. Standing on the opposite bank, Orlando and others waved to me. Federico, the most elegant old man and probably stronger than anybody, gestured with one forearm to a good place for me to cross the water. After a long drink, I heaved my pack back on and trudged over. I was getting to like crossing these rivers in clothes and boots.

Rio Sussio was our most rustic camp to date. Mighty stones defined the river bank, and jungle sprang up directly behind. No flies on our tribe—even in the dark, machetes were hacking in minutes, clearing ground for the tents. Stacy and Brett, cheated of the sympathy heat stroke victims deserve, decided to move stones and pitch their tent apart from everyone, farther down the narrow beach.

Dinner was nearly impossible to arrange, in the pitch darkness with bags of miscellaneous kitchen equipment strewn willy-nilly amongst the rocks. Usually we made camp early enough to organize under the last bit of daylight. Tonight everyone was shattered from the day's output, while every light was employed getting the tents and shelters up. Ever aware of the morale-boosting property of a hot meal after a wreck of a day, Orlando (immune to fatigue) calmly rolled up his sleeves, and out of thin air pulled a vat of hot spaghetti and tuna. Even Carmela stood back dumbfounded, not sure how he swung it. Sometimes Orlando's spirit, good will, and energy nourished the whole camp.

∿

DAY TEN

FROM FEDERICO OR EL CASSIKE, WE KNEW how many hours or days away the communities were. But, aside from Federico's one-family farm in Bajo Relibo and the three families in Sley, there were only two other "villages" in all of Karakima. Now we were en route to Alto Relibo, the biggest settlement, at the top of the Relibo River.

We knew Day Ten was going to be a wipe out. We were going over Aguila. 'Aguila' means 'eagle,' and Eagle Mountain would be higher than anything we'd climbed. The day before, from a wide place in the Rio Relibo, Federico had pointed to Aguila up in the distance. And again through an open patch in the green jungle wall we'd seen just her summit. Apparently this overall range reached ten thousand feet (about two miles up) somewhere between Alto Relibo village and Cielo Grande, our destination near the Pacific coast. But numbers weren't the language here, steepness was. The only way to get to where the rest of the Locandia people dwelled was over this mountain. And Federico, The Cassike, and everyone we'd asked, said it would be two hours straight up.

Again I woke on the wrong side of my sleeping bag, mainly because Orlando had had the light on from twelve-thirty to one-thirty, then aroused us at three-fifty to commence the day. Since we all knew we wouldn't leave camp till eleven, his eccentricities were beyond irksome. I grumbled to myself through the morning, and even my daily dunk in the purifying waters didn't clear the irritation.

Brett's tenacity about dragging phenomenal amounts of equipment everywhere was wearing on not only my common sense, but finally Orlando's. Yet no amount of sensible discourse, nor the sight of struggling men under massive loads, could convince Brett that we weren't a Red Cross unit. Stacy backed him all the way. But Aguila would be too intense for anyone to carry crazy loads. And there was no one else around to hire. So, once again, the only solution was to leave Brett and Stacy behind and continue the nonsensical exercise of sending men back the next day. "What's the point of dragging around all these emergency aids," I asked Orlando, "if Brett and the emergency aids are always a day behind us somewhere?" We were becoming two expeditions, or one with a bulky shadow. Meanwhile Brett and Stacy were missing all the adventure of the unknown and the arrivals to where the tribal people were. "I do feel kind of sorry for them," I added.

Orlando eyed me strangely, "Are you crazy? They having a great time..." He paused to let me imagine being madly in love with someone in this divine setting...and how blissful it could be to wave bye-bye to all of us each morning then honeymoon naked by the river in the tropical sun all day. Plus this was their first trip outside the U.S. "Feel sorry for us," Orlando suggested, "because we always waiting for them."

To drive home the point to Brett that we HAD to do this journey with the number of men we now had (additional help no longer existed), I had decided to carry more weight myself. The day before, I'd carried an orange rubber washing basin (strapped to my back like a tortoise shell) and Ernesto's sleeping bag because he'd been so overloaded. Today I'd carry my sleeping bag, my usual pack with journal and camera stuff and emergency gear, plus all my clothing— maybe forty pounds total, double my usual. As I loaded up, Orlando approached me in disbelief. "You don't take this extra bag," he warned.

"Yes, I'm taking it. I'll be alright," I answered, unconvincingly.

"Why? You don't need those clothes. They come tomorrow with Brett."

"I can manage it," I told Orlando, deliberately avoiding the 'why' part of his query.

He tried to talk me out of it; but there was another reason I didn't want to leave anything behind. Tomas would be departing from Alto Relibo, at the top of Mount Aguila, and there was a fair chance that the last minute I'd scram with him. It completely depended on how things went between Orlando and me. Since we were only carrying crucial cargo today, like kitchen accoutrements, tents, and Tomas's photography crates—not my extra clothing—I'd have to carry it myself. I'd hoped to do it more discreetly. But, as I mentioned, nothing goes unseen in intimate settings like ours, and my nonchalantly grabbing an extra twenty pounds before heading up this monster mountain did not compute. Tomas would be leaving before Brett and Stacy caught up with us, though, so I needed everything with me if I was to exit with him.

Fool move. The weight was insane. As well as my usual backpack, waist-pack, and sleeping bag, I was now handicapped by this other heavy bag over one shoulder. From the onset I knew I was in trouble. Aguila was ferocious. And the additional bag not only put me off balance but employed my free hand, sorely needed today. In the other hand was my trusty walking stick.

But no one could help me since each of the men already had over eighty pounds.

Aguila began just inches from our campsite, at about an eighty-five degree angle. Due to the encasing foliage, I couldn't see any of the others, but knew by the pace we'd grown accustomed to that they were long gone. So I was soon solo, clinging to the mountain in fatigued frustration and cursing my stupidity.

We'd endured a few trials by now; and most of the fears such as slipping, falling, getting lost, bitten by a snake, or swallowed by a tiger, had taken a back seat to the absolute concentration required to move with speed, skill, and strength. But on Aguila, the intensity never let up. Over and over and over, again and again and again, one had to lift oneself up, grasping vines and roots for leverage, clutching at whatever plant could be safely grasped, and pitting one's weight against the tenacity of its root-hold, hauling oneself ever higher—a human pulley. The choice not to subject oneself to this was noticeably absent, so we were all stuck with the problem (familiar of late) of having to continue when we weren't sure we had the stuff.

I was not only in short supply of strength and courage, but overly endowed with material stuff. Somewhere behind me, others were laboring too—Carmela, Cappy, and the guys with the hugest and most unwieldy loads. When we looked at each other's faces, the eyes stayed fixed in the black focus of the struggle, sweat on the eyelashes and chin. There was no additional energy for the softening of the eyes or a smile. Your own anguish was mirrored to you, and that was the extent of sympathy. This upward motion, denying both thought and precaution, would continue all the way to the summit. In my deepest soul, I didn't see how I could make it.

Halfway up, I fell upon Orlando and the faster climbers, all collapsed wearily in the undergrowth, a beaten lot, sucking oranges from Sley, with their packs scattered amongst stones and trees. I flopped to the ground, avoiding eye contact, and looked in the other direction. Being a wimp was a confusing feeling, and I was torn between being a man and being a woman. It would be such an unfair moment to expect one of the men to take on my extra bag. My spirit was down, thanks to Orlando's pre-dawn exuberance and Brett's stubborn insistence on medical security—both men were driving everyone a little crazy. So, with my sweaty back to everyone, I just sat and discreetly wept. Since I was the only one here who could get away with it, I couldn't pass up the opportunity.

But I felt lousy for cracking—I was hardly the only one having a rough time. Did I have any right to break? Were they all as bent to the limit as me, or did their upper body strength equip them better for this? I was definitely getting signals from my lower center of gravity that this was truly too strenuous. Right here on the side of this mountain I was finally putting my finger on the real difference between men and women. For me now there was an element of risk, possibly something to lose if I didn't honor my limits. But that risk didn't seem present in the men. They had reserves or something deep in their abdomens, where I had...empty space.

Eventually I heard everyone moving off, up the mountain. And when I turned around a few moments later, no one was there.

And neither was my yellow bag.

One of the guys had saved me, I didn't know who. But I'd be forever grateful, that was certain. Without a word, someone had totally covered me, taking that extra weight himself, halfway up this torturous mountain, and added it to his already-immense load...

So I now made my way onward, still battling for every foot of altitude, but tremendously relieved without that extra weight. Stomping along later, about two-thirds of the way up, I was wondering what on Earth does this sort of thing prepare you for? Only two answers came: childbirth or another expedition. I paused and waited a moment for Carmela, who stayed near me at times like this. She puffed to a halt behind me. "Carmela, is childbirth easier than this or harder?"

"Oh, easier," she panted. "In childbirth you start five in the morning and by seven-thirty you got ba-a-by..." her eyes lit up. "Up here, you start five in the morning and by twelve noon you got NOTHIN'."

Aguila Mountain was the ultimate. Two hours straight up, with cargo. But we made it! (Every day up here we seemed to surpass our previous limit.) At the top, it began to rain.

The plan had been to go down the back side of Aguila to Rio Tongo and camp there. Thankfully, Aguila's other side had a much gentler angle, so I loped along in the rain, Carmela behind me, knowing the others were up ahead some-where, and a few were behind us somewhere. And I sang a happy song because Aguila was now, for each of us, an achievement.

With the mornings clear, we'd been striving for early departures, but hadn't once left camp before eleven—partly because the a.m. sunshine offered the only occasion to dry clothing and partly because the excess cargo required so much discussion, debate, and now arguing. But trekking in the torrents was dangerous, and dark since we were two to three canopies below the sun. And of course the mud situation was making the clothing situation worse. The clothing situation was a mess. Pants were splitting and shirts were torn on thorns. Socks were now loose netting, boots always saturated, all packs heavier than ever with all the contents wet.

As we trotted down Aguila, it began to pour, but of course we kept moving. Carmela and I figured camp was just a little farther down the way. We continued figuring that for the next three hours. Up ahead, unbeknownst to us, Federico, the fifty-seven-year-old goat who knew every undulation of the mountain, had again suggested we go all the way. With our full caravan stretching out over a mile, all the rear element could do was keep hiking until camp was finally stumbled upon.

. . . . . .

There was never anything along the path in the way of people, dwellings, litter, shopping centers. Nothing. Ever. Just untouched jungle—seemingly endless in all directions, including up and down. Far above, somewhere beyond the canopy layers, and making little difference to us, was the sky, that would begin darkening around noon and break open within a few hours. On the muddy ground underfoot was the underworld of crawly things: five-inch centipedes coiled in circles, ants of all sizes busily going places in lines (I hereby decree that there are more ants in the world than probably anything else), lots of flying bugs with pretty designs on their heads or backs landing or taking off as we tore through their neighborhoods, gorgeous butterflies, including one variety with an eight-inch wing-span of metallic blue underneath and aluminum silver on top. Breathtaking and abundant. Lots of bird song, but we saw few of the singers. Birds kept their distance because every man (we and the Indians) carried a rifle and used it on absolutely anything. We saw surprisingly few animals other than insects, though, probably because they heard us coming. The plant life was consistent as we moved through, no marked diversity from one mountain to the next. Almost all the flowers and berrylike fruits that grew wild were red or red-orange. And red was the sign of being poisonous. We touched nothing we didn't easily recognize, though all the Costa Ricans, including Orlando (who'd traveled in many Central American jungles), were far more plant-literate than we gringos. But we were learning fast. The trees were mammoth, undisturbed it seemed for hundreds of years, and stretching with all their might for that veiled sun overhead. Often we'd find them uprooted, possibly lifeless for years, sometimes by a river, or just in the woods—the diameter of their root base sometimes wider than thirty feet.

None of this could be photographed for three reasons. One, it was so dark that I couldn't get a light-reading. Two, whenever we were in the deep jungle, we were rapidly moving. Occasionally at a rest stop there'd be something remarkable, but the third reason usually cancelled rest-stop photography, too: the constant rain. The dreary showers made things darker still. And with all the river crossings and daily deluges penetrating our packs, one hesitated to expose camera, film, and lenses to even more water.

We trudged on in the rain. Whenever we reached a river now—they seemed to be everywhere—we'd simply pause for breath, glance across for the best fording place, and plow across. We were wet all the time. Higher up now, it was also cold. Our yellow ponchos (supplied by Jesse, and part of everyone's cargo), that we all opened like parachutes at the first drop each day, offered protection but only to a point. Our packs, underneath, would eventually soak through. Our clothing was already saturated from sweat and rivers, our feet muddy to the ankles, and our socks squishing inside our boots like sponges. But we would continue...climbing, jumping, pulling ourselves up over mossy, ant-ridden tree-trunks, through thickets, and under low-hanging vines.

Today, for the first time, we passed a few Indians on the trail. Because the jungle absorbs all sound, we found ourselves face-to-face with them all of a sudden, the darkness and teeming rain further dramatizing the encounters. Until today, we didn't even know anyone else traversed the jungle—so deep is it, and vast as space. And they, of course, were even more shocked to behold the likes of us. Like beings from Jupiter meeting beings from Saturn halfway in between the two planets, we'd all stop and stare at each other, then half-smile then continue in our opposite directions.

The first Indian we saw was a barefoot mother with a baby on her back and a banana leaf on top to keep the rain off the child. Behind her was a young boy, also barefoot, with three piglets on a leash. Later, we passed a couple—he with a load on his back, she with a load and baby on hers—and behind them a young child with his own huge load. These people, and supposedly lots of other Indians (Federico had informed Orlando who parlayed it to us) were on their way to a party—the big do of the year, down in Sley.

Just before dark, a final grand ascent led us to—the last thing we expected—a huge pasture covering two complete hilltops, and speckled with seven happy cows. In the jungle, you don't get views—you climb and climb, but even the summits are encased in foliage. From up here, though, we could see everything—all the mountains we'd crossed! With shrouds of fog draping the hills in an uneven pattern, this was like some far-away retreat where you go to purify and heal your soul.

We had reached Alto Relibo. A long thatched house adjoined the pasture, and in it was an easy-going, elderly Indian woman, as well as the advance members of our tribe. But before joining them, I dropped my load and climbed the grassy hill rising way above the jungle world below. After today's work-out, this moist, expansive, tranquilizing vista provided restorative energy. Tomas came with me, both of us mesmerized by the serene grandeur of the spacious green universe surrounding us. It was uplifting to experience distance again. The jungle is such a world of proximity, its message all about nearness, that you subconsciously begin to disbelieve there's anything outside it. Now our jungle sprawled below in all directions. We stood inhaling the clouds, watching their film create changing Japanese landscapes around us. We just stayed there, awestruck and reverent, until the light was almost gone.

Then, recalling the expedition we were on, we ran down the hill to help get the tents up before nightfall.

Beaming from a pile of cargo beside the thatched hut, I spied my bright yellow bag, "Who carried it?" I meekly asked Wilfredo, feeling truly awful about the whole episode.

"Orlando," said Wilfredo.

WOULD CHELA'S PROPHECY of unfriendly natives come true? Orlando had said he wanted none of such talk. And by now I was on his wavelength, come what may. The lady of the long thatched hut was pleasant enough and donated the bigger portion of it to us (surely in exchange for Orlando's cash). Perfect because now we had roomy, comfy shelter for cooking, could live more like the "locals," and avoid the rain. For sleeping, we'd still use our tents.

Our diet now, like the jungle people, was almost exclusively bananas and plantain. The only other available foods were oranges and limes, and they were down in Bajo Relibo, not up here. To vary things, we also cooked our rice and beans mornings and evenings, continually amazed at how good they could taste each time. And today Orlando procured a pig, so there was meat for a couple of days (that I, of course, avoided). All other rations we'd used up, except the onions and garlic we'd brought plenty of. On the trail we sometimes found and cut sugar cane, a timely treat. I felt healthy and fine; and the others seemed well. Bananas and plantain, it is said, are among the few foods you can subsist on exclusively.

Day Eleven. Orlando, Federico, El Cassike, Tomas, Elieser, and I went to explore the tribal community while the others stayed on the hilltop resting and washing and drying clothes. This was the moment we'd looked forward to, meeting the most remote people in Costa Rica.

With Federico and The Cassike greeting each family personally, it definitely took the edge off our intrusion. The Cassike, it appeared, was quite the hero around here. Orlando said that whenever he'd gone anywhere alone with The Cassike, they'd been treated extremely well. Apparently this guy was respected, appreciated, and seen by all as a kind of messenger-slash-communicator. It wasn't customary up here to "get around" the way he did, bringing news from hither and yon. Orlando said these people probably viewed him as a dashing, romantic figure.

I had to giggle—to me he maintained an impenetrable air of seriousness. Also, he had the disturbing habit of disappearing out on the trail. Whenever he wasn't in the lead, he seemed to enjoy a little game of blazing new trails, looking for short cuts. Occasionally we'd arrive at a river or mountaintop and he'd already be there waiting. More often, though, Orlando would have to stop the whole group in hopes that The Cassike would somehow rejoin us, though he generally didn't. Instead, we'd eventually move on only to find later that he'd silently rematerialized in our midst. Thus his nickname, The Vanishing Cassike.

Our arrival in Alto Relibo made curious headlines, since we were such a crazy racial mix. Several of our group were part Indian themselves, Orlando was black (in keeping with the general ethnicity of the Central American east coast) and Tomas and I were white. The rest of our group were black, Spanish origin, Indian, or any combination thereof.

Today, as we went from one dwelling to another, Indians from the previous household would reappear in the next one, talking in low tones to a son or daughter, snickering or just staring. We had now actually eased gradually much closer into their way of life—from San Jose to Punta del Sol to Truluka to Federico's. In these last eleven days we'd actually been living more or less the way they did, becoming intimate with the limitations and advantages of their rain forest. So their tribal ways did not seem to us so outlandish or even fascinating at this point. And rather than being boggled at how they could live so simply, we were awestruck by their luxuries—shelter, fires, sleeping nests…

Curiously, it felt natural, even nice, to just stare at each other. We would arrive at a hut and just look around, and they'd sit or stand or lean and watch us in return. And despite what it had taken us to get there, the fact was, they were more dumbfounded by us than we by them. And when the rain began and we, as one, produced and donned our yellow rubber ponchos, they looked at each other then all burst into laughter.

The Locandia People: Their homes are always on land that's been cleared of dense jungle; and banana and cacao have been planted as crops. The construction of huts consists of four wooden poles as corners, and palm or other fronds woven into an elegant rain-proof roof. No walls. Inside many of the huts are little lofts built of either bark or bamboo poles tied together for a loft floor; these protected spaces are for storing bananas or 'chicha' (their alcoholic corn beverage) or for sleeping children. For a staircase, they cut notches into a slim tree-trunk and lean it against the loft floor—as we'd seen before. All the huts have dirt floors and are generally dark inside, mainly due to the high contrast of the brilliant sun outside and the generous frond overhangs protecting everyone from the rain. The smaller huts are lighter inside. Animals wander freely in and out— roosters and chicks and hens laying eggs on piles of clothing, pigs and piglets scratching their backs against carved wooden stools, scrawny dogs and puppies sniffing and cavorting with the other animals, all the creatures poking around for food. There are children everywhere, all ages. Every woman has an infant on her back or at her breast, or she's pregnant, or both. The adult faces are handsome, but unkempt. Smiles are hidden. Eyes slow to soften. The people are proud, not intimidated by whatever it is we have and they don't. We've come to them, after all.

As we went along from hut to hut, Orlando told them simply, through The Cassike or Federico, that we'd come to see how they lived, to find out more about them, and to try to learn from them. He asked all possible questions about their food, their herbal cures, their tools, their religion, and beliefs. Most of the men spoke Spanish and some were relaxed and ready to talk, others more reticent. The women hung back, murmuring together in the Locandia tongue, many nursing babies and stirring the big pot on the inside fire that burned continually in each hut.

The flames were kept alight by four to seven logs (as long as twelve or fifteen feet) whose ends came together as an asterisk, and were lit in that center. The logs radiated out across the hut floors. To rekindle the flames, someone would simply shove the longest log or two inward another foot, and voila. So ingenious, so easy, so functional. The fires never went out.

A lot of the huts had hammocks where babies were rocking during the day. All the children were filthy, as were the adults, generally. Most were barefoot and many had weeks or years of mud and insect bites on their legs and feet. They wore western clothing, apparently a recent adaptation. All girls and women wore skirts and dresses and possessed probably only one outfit each. Their clothes were dirty and ragged. Here and there a person had on black rubber loafers. The only other footwear was the standard black rubber ankle boot that they all wore for trekking around. The women wore cheap beads, but not handcrafted locally; they'd been acquired probably from down-river and maybe restrung with other beads previously scored. They secured their babies to their backs in a piece of cloth tied tightly just above their sagging breasts. The women were ageless. Some were over fifty, the rest, who knows? Orlando said many of the mothers were just teenagers. Every female was a mother, a child, or both.

"What do these people do all day?" I asked Orlando, as we moved from one hut to another. "They're always just sitting in their houses when we arrive."

"Their life is in the jungle," he replied. "That is what it's all about for them, their challenge." (But viewing my photos later, I could see the reticence and apprehension in the Indian faces, and realized they were sitting in their houses today waiting for 'the invaders' to show up. They all knew we'd arrived the previous night, and they were gripped with misgivings as The Cassike, Federico, three strange men, and one blonde, blue-eyed *gringa* came a-knockin'.)

For us, the senses were reeling. I was fulfilled to observe and take photos...memorizing what I could. Orlando was ingesting everything possible, artifactually and religiously, finally uncovering for himself what he'd been dreaming of since he was a little boy staring off into the distant fog-covered mountains of Karakima. His conversations with Federico and others, though, were always in Spanish, and with so much happening so fast, little was translated for me. I was getting more than I could manage, though, through the eyes alone.

All in all, we were well received. We weren't offered 'chicha,' the cordial corn drink male guests are customarily served, but we didn't want any, by the looks of it.

Even up here in the community, there was a lot of climbing to do between huts, so we were on the move all day. Then, afterwards, we ventured down to the river for a plunge and some restful moments of warming ourselves in the sun on huge hot boulders in the shallows.

When we got back to the old lady's long thatched hut, Carmela had already cooked supper and even folded the clothes we'd washed that morning. (But the stains of jungle residue are fairly indelible).

There were fifteen of us tonight, a solid group with good cooperation and a sense of unity. It was a toasty feeling, coming in out of the rain after a mud-slide day of many sensations, to just sit by the fire and drink hot tea made from lime leaves Orlando had picked. This, we hoped, would be the core group to continue our journey.

With the exception of Tomas, who was leaving the next morning… Four men would accompany him, carrying his photographic equipment and baggage. They'd walk two days to San Felipe. From San Felipe, Tomas would try to get a ride to Turrialba, then a bus to San Jose, then fly to New York. We'd miss him, but he had a deadline, and all the delays had swallowed up his time. So I gave him a letter for Darcy, who was probably back from New York by now and waiting for word from us in San Jose.

"You the official photographer now," Orlando said to me. "Make sure Tomas show you how to work the film before he go." Tomas and I smiled at each other.

The next morning, as Tomas finished posing with everyone who wanted to have Polaroids taken with him, I hugged him tightly. What a way to get to know someone. Sometimes you wonder, when you make a new friend, how they'd measure up in a pinch, what kind of depth they had. Tomas was as good as they come. I kissed him goodbye and couldn't hold back a few tears. As he headed off north, or east, or toward some hills we hadn't climbed, the rest of us got ready for the journey back down the river. Day Twelve was going to be another of pushing our limits. We felt up to it though.

❧

PART III - U-TURN

DAY TWELVE

THE ORIGINAL PLAN HAD BEEN to try to continue on through the mountains beyond Alto Relibo, and reach Cielo Grande that way. But now that we were here, it was confirmed that no trail existed. The only way to Cielo Grande, or any place over on the Pacific side, was through a 'village' called San Locandi. If we wanted to try to get through, San Locandi was the only possible starting place. But good luck!

San Locandi, however, was all the way back down the way we'd come up—back down Aguila, back to Sley, even back to Federico's farm—then across a land-mass between two rivers. On my 'map'—that I'd drawn by hand based on what people in Truluka had been able to communicate—this village was a dot on that land-mass. From there we'd go to another river, the Rio Enok, that we'd have to travel up as we had just done along Rio Relibo. At the top of the Rio Enok, supposedly Indians had been known to go all the way through the mountains to Cielo Grande, near the Pacific coast.

Our key mission had been to come up to Alto Relibo to see the tribal people, but Orlando was still determined to go all the way to Cielo Grande, no matter what or how. And despite the overages of time and money. This meant we'd definitely have to move faster, since we'd now be back-tracking several days' worth of jungle. If it took us eleven days to get this far, it could take *forever* to get through to the west coast, unless we shifted gears.

We'd sent a message to Brett—via some Alto Relibo Indians heading down to the party at Sley—that they should wait for us at the Rio Sussio camp instead of coming up to Alto Relibo with all the equipment. (It was actually a good thing we couldn't penetrate the jungle up here to continue west, because none of the guys, *none*, was willing to go back down for Brett and the stuff, then climb back up Aguila.)

Day Twelve was the beginning of a different mind-set. And, with not a word about it, the fifteen of us in Alto Relibo all knew. From here, we wouldn't be thinking about culture or anthropology or fascinating flora. We wouldn't be learning the jungle ways or soaking up the novelty of the experience. We'd be thinking about distance. Whatever was slowing us down would be overcome.

So, instead of sending guys back down for Brett today, we'd all go back down. Interesting as the people were in Alto Relibo, they were not unlike those in Sley and Bajo Relibo, and it wasn't essential to spend more time up here. Plus we'd visit more families in San Locandi. Anyway, it was turning out that we learned more about the Indians and their lives by traveling through their jungle and battling nature as they did than by standing around watching them watching us in their huts. The hiking was what brought us closer to them. And, as far as they were concerned, the fact that we'd appeared here at all, in their remote village, could only mean we'd climbed for days through rain and mud and camped in the jungle…that we were strong.

We were strong. We'd continually amazed ourselves by what we were capable of, and now we were actually kind of addicted to the work-outs and the daily awe factor. Whenever we spent a day in camp without trekking, we'd be chomping at the bit to get back out there to sweat and strain again. We'd built up our endurance and felt physically prepared now for just about anything.

Day Twelve, Orlando suggested we high-tail it down to Rio Sussio (going down that front face of Aguila had to be easier than coming up), grab Brett, Stacy, and the stuff (we had more Indians to help now, who were off to Sley anyway), then push on, all together, all the way back to Federico's farm in Bajo Relibo. It had taken us about eleven hours total to travel that distance coming up here, but we'd move faster today, and we'd save an hour or more by going down Aguila, not up.

This was unanimously agree to, *con gusto*. The fifteen of us felt a splendid self-sufficient lightness without all the equipment and afflictions surrounding Brett and Stacy. This posse seemed fit to undertake the rest of the trip.

After marching around with the Indians the last few days, with women and children as well as men, we'd picked up some of their climbing techniques—you sort of had to, and fast, or they were gone. A nice little assist for our jaunt down to Bajo Relibo was a fancy new step we'd learned. I called it "the Alto Relibo Scoot" (to myself, since I didn't know the Spanish or Locandia word for 'scoot'). To describe this traveling method, I can only compare it to 'skiing.' You have a pole (walking stick) in one hand, or a huge machete—that all the natives carry, including seven-year-old girls—and with that for balance on your turns, you banish all thought and FLY down the trail behind the person in front of you. Your eyes leave the ground for fractions of seconds only, and rarely; your undivided attention is downward and forward. If someone speaks behind you, chances are you'll slip—even listening breaks the concentration. The entire human chain whips down the curves, cargo strapped to backs, mud gushing under black rubber boots, minds empty. The Alto Relibo Scoot is a fabulous sport. (Uphill is the same mind-set but obviously slower.) And there is no stopping at all except for intentional and cherished rest stops about every hour and a half.

The path from Alto to Bajo Relibo had been used by Indians for thousands of years. Some of the Locandias with us probably could've flown it blindfolded. The children were fearless. And, I dare say, our little crowd did a commendable job, too, ripping right along with them. In fact,

I'm certain they intended to leave us in a mud slide some-where—they were full of condescending mischief as we set out—but were amazed they couldn't shake us. This was just one of those places in the world where there's no such thing as a wimp; and within a few hours we were one tight tribe, having a whale of a time.

Teaming up with different segments of our original group, at intervals during the day, I saw that everyone had mastered the scoot…wild abandon with your eyes ahead of your feet, simply entrusting those feet to somehow catch up. But where the feet failed, the backside came in handy. And when you broke concentration and did slip, as happened to everyone including Indians at least once every day or two, you bounced back to your feet like a rub-ber ball. I don't know whether the intense mind-set kept us from getting hurt or whether we did get hurt but didn't have time to acknowledge it. I think it was originally the latter and evolved into the former. Either way, the power of the mind was always making itself known to us.

At this exhilarating pace, we reached Rio Sussio in just three and a half hours, and scooted all the way down Aguila in forty-five minutes! Of course the descent was en-tirely encased in foliage, so we never knew how near the bottom we were, except for the rising volume of the river below. And the camp was right at the base of the sheer mountain, so as we came thrashing into camp, we'd have to really jam on the brakes or end up in the river.

But the river looked like a perfect landing place to me, so I didn't stop.

Scooting was so enthralling that all of us, Indians in-cluded, were utterly giddy after three and a half hours of it. And as we crashed into the quiet camp, winded and laughing, Stacy and Brett couldn't suss our delirium. They thought what they'd missed was arduous torture, until we returned, one huge tribe covered in mud and lost in mirth. Also, unbeknownst to them, we'd be continuing another six hours, so this was but a rest stop and we didn't intend to lose momentum. I could tell by the ambiance in the camp—a quiet sunny morning by the river—that our pace would throw Brett and Stacy for a major loop when they joined us in a short while.

After a swim and some rice and beans, we crossed the river and leaped up the next mountain, at least ten Locandias now helping us with cargo. Stacy and Brett, though they set out with us, weren't seen again until two hours after the rest of us arrived back at Federico's.

One of the day's many highlights was the lucky timing of passing through Sley again as the big gala was winding into its second day. Gathered in one of the three huts were about fifty or more Indians from the entire region. When we arrived, they were dancing in a circle to the sound of a wobbly tape, and drinking chicha. Dogs and babies were as numerous here as in their homes.

At the sight of us, the Indians stopped dancing and stood back for a good long stare. Everyone by now had either met us, seen us, or heard about us. Stand-offish at first, they soon came over to the wooden fence where we were observing with decorum, and offered cups of chicha to the men. I tried to look thirsty (which wasn't hard) because I was dying for a taste of this drink, but they weren't about to relinquish the age-old tradition of only serving males. Four or five of the men did shake my hand quite sweetly and smiled shyly at all of us. It was invitational and heart-warming—a genuine acceptance, now that we'd shown our lack of malice and surprising fortitude.

With my short, short hair with a braided tail down the neck, and my boyish frame, I knew I was a focal point for the Indians. I was the only white person in our group of more than twenty, the only one with blue eyes, and the only woman (since Carmela, shocking one and all, had marched on ahead solo and hadn't been seen since Rio Sussio). Despite my distinctions, the Indians concealed their curiosity well. But, again, they were experts at looking away just in time— polite shyness a way of life.

Even amongst our tribe I saw that shyness. Where Americans or Europeans would yank off their clothes and plunge naked into a mountain stream, or at least find a secluded area then strip down for a bath, these Costa Ricans chose the most public spot for bathing and left their underwear on. If I happened to be nearby—often that had to be the case—they gave me complete privacy from even just a few feet away. For all of us, bathing was catch as catch can. There was so much to do in camp (we were constantly preparing for the next day's walk or recovering from the last one), that to grab a thorough head-to-toe you really had to steal away, and there was rarely time. Orlando, in the same orderly fashion he did everything, intelligently attended to these restorative pleasures at dawn, along with his prayer. And Ernesto had a way of sometimes disappearing into the night after dinner and returning shiny and smelling like soap.

Shyness and humility, I learned, are components of the Costa Rican national character. The more relaxed I was about being a woman, the shyer the men were. And when I acted like one of the guys, they treated me like one of the guys. They teased and flirted and joked about me, among themselves all the time, and they all had asked Tomas to take Polaroids of me standing next to them, but to date, other than gentlemanly offerings like carrying my load, carving me a cork, cutting me a walking stick, or peeling sugar cane for me, no advances had been made. One day, while we were camped at Federico's the first time, Tomas had passed Cappy and Elieser's little shelter and seen them carefully combing their hair and taking turns holding that little broken piece of mirror that was hanging luxuriously in the hut. Laughing, Tomas had asked why on Earth they were concerned about how they looked out here. "For Wendy," they'd both answered…and Tomas, of course, reported straight back to me. So, I *was* recognized as female, but they never let me know. Being Orlando's sister-in-law surely separated me, too.

Had we not been so exhausted and still one and a half hours from completing the day's hike, we may have dallied at the party in Sley, but we had to press on. It was getting late, and Orlando was the only one who fancied jungle-stomping by flashlight. Moving off from the festivities, I stayed with Ernesto, who'd been farther behind all day due to an unusually heavy load.

Arriving at a tributary of the river, I was sticking to my new (and short-lived) resolution of taking shoes off before fording rivers. (If the boots never dried, I imagined they might disintegrate on some mountain pass later. But they never dried anyway with the rain and mud.) Once my boots were off, I was tempted to take a full plunge. "Let's swim," I tried a little Spanish on my companion.

"My back. Is too hot," Ernesto answered, trying a little English. And I wondered how he could resist these crystal mountain streams that Orlando and I indulged in several times a day. I peeled off the trousers, and left on the soaking T-shirt and undies, my standard bathing attire for mixed company out here. The cold water covered me, entered every pore, and flowed right through me. I stayed under, watching the white-green bubbles of the gushing little waterfall above me. So rejuvenating was the coolness that I lingered there, bracing myself against the current by holding onto boulders, until the heat had left every artery, vein, joint, and bone. Coming up, I didn't look at Ernesto. I slipped out of the stream with my back to him, took off the T-shirt, and wrung it out so it would dry quicker and be less transparent. When I put it back on and faced him, he was respectfully turned the other way.

We then crossed over with our packs and sat on the rocks on the other side, to put our boots back on. Any tourist or lover would've somehow capitalized on this little scene. I wondered what my Costa Rican friend would do... To my delight, he stayed there with me, quietly sitting on a rock, maybe feeling, like I did, that this was the first and possibly last time we'd ever be alone. The sound of the rushing stream engulfed everything, and we shared a few long moments of not talking, partly because we couldn't and partly because we had nothing to say. Neither of us seemed to want to get going, so we simply stayed there, waiting for nothing. Then suddenly Orlando appeared on the opposite bank with Federico, two young boys, and a fat unhappy pig on a rope. Tomorrow the pig would interrupt our banana diet, today they all interrupted a sweet moment.

"What are you doing?" Orlando asked, arriving on our side of the stream. He had a way of not giving you the benefit of the doubt.

"We're waiting for Brett," I answered, while Ernesto probably wondered whether we really were waiting for Brett.

We continued to wait for Brett, and to watch the boys poking and jabbing the poor pig across the water with sticks while Orlando put his socks and boots back on (he had made the shoes-off resolution also, only to break it shortly). Standing up, he faced us, "Are you going to stay here and wait or are you going to come with me?" He occasionally had traces of a little boy who didn't like doing things without the whole gang. He tarried slightly.

"We'll come with you," I said, getting up, and smiling at Ernesto.

"You might wait all night for Brett," Orlando said, and off we marched.

Seeing Federico's thatched roof snug in the greenery was a cozy sight. We'd left Alto Relibo at 8:15 a.m. and it was now 5:45. Filthy and aching, it felt oddly like coming home. We'd spent three or four nights here before and now we were back. Joyfully, we swarmed in and got the fire and beans going. What made it even sweeter was that Carmela had preceded everyone and was bathed and cheerful and ready to make a huge feast for us.

❧

DAY THIRTEEN. THE PLAN HAD BEEN to leave at dawn for San Locandi. But as we guzzled coffee, Cappy suggested we hold here a day. His point, a delicate matter, was that we could not complete this challenging quest with all this junk—some things had to be left behind. Another delay was anything but ideal, but after the output of Day Twelve, Day Thirteen could be well spent resting and sorting paraphernalia.

Cappy, as a Captain or Lieutenant or whatever he was, was the spokesman for the Costa Rican men. He was now saying that Orlando and Brett would have to work something out together because the other men, from here on, would only carry essential cargo. No more nonsense.

Learning now that all the guys shared my strong views on the subject, I avoided the situation and spent a quiet day washing clothes, writing, and enjoying the beauty of Federico's farm. It was lovely to be part of such a nice community of people. Who would imagine that a group of seventeen or eighteen (or however many there were in our core group, not counting the Indians that came in for a day or two, but counting the ones that stayed with us like Federico and The Cassike) could coexist so easily with so little? The project at hand tightly bound us. Individual motivation was high. We were weaving a tale, building more strength than we thought we had, and living a complete fantasy in which no one could guess what lay ahead.

That night a light rain fell and most everyone went to sleep early. Huddling under the thatched over-hang of the *rancho*, Orlando, Chela, and I ate a fish Orlando had cooked and listened to tales of his romance with Darcy.

~ May 30, 1985 — Bajo Relibo

DAY FOURTEEN

DAY FOURTEEN. UP AT FIVE O'CLOCK—Orlando wishing he hadn't overslept. Blue fog hugging the little valley but quickly lifting. We were now more organized; Cappy had divided the guys into four groups who would, from now on, rotate the kitchen chores. Coffee was ready at six rather than eight-thirty.

After a full day in camp the previous day, everyone was eager to hit the trail. And, one more time, heading out today felt like the real beginning of the adventure. We didn't know what to expect from here—we may not see a living soul from San Locandi to Cielo Grande. We'd already found that the few settlements indicated on the maps of this region were usually just a couple of families. But from San Locandi to Cielo Grande there were no settlements on the maps, just 10,000 foot mountains and sources of several rivers. But we were ready. Fear and doubt about both the trip and the leadership were behind us. Conquering Aguila, arriving in the Alto Relibo Shangri-la, being accepted by the Indians and sliding wildly through the mud with them, were unprecedented joys. If the rest was sheer hell, we'd still be forever enriched from these last few days.

Orlando now told us straight that it was going to be tough, and no one balked. A hot meal and a circle of smiles seemed enough to balance the duress.

The Cassike said there were tigers up there and that from today we'd have to tighten the ranks. I'd sensed that in the jungle the animals sought to avoid humans completely and that, although we didn't see them, they saw us. Back in Punta del Sol, Orlando had said, "The jungle like women— women are safe there." Today he said, "I made a mistake when I tell you that thing… The Cassike tell me the tiger like the women best."

"Don't tell that to Stacy or Carmela," I advised him. Many a time Carmela or I had found ourselves totally alone, often for hours at a time. Would the men now keep an eye on us?

Snakes, too, had moved farther from mind recently, maybe because the Alto Relibo trail was well-trodden. But Gregorio had already killed one Terciopelo ('Fer-de-Lance' in English and French)—a deadly snake that calls Costa Rica home—and Federico had a disabled finger from a bite earlier in life. What I didn't know then is that the Terciopelo is not only profuse in Karakima but has venom to spare, making it particularly aggressive. And the females give birth to litters of babies, not eggs, numbering ten to eighty snakes. Like the other jungle fauna, maybe the snakes kept their distance from humans. After San Locandi, though, we were going where there were no people. "Don't think about snakes," warned Orlando. "Those thoughts attract them. I never think about them and they don't show themself to me."

Meanwhile, we had a two-day walk ahead of us, to San Locandi.

~ May 31, 1985 — Bajo Relibo

. . . . . .

Drama.

Just as we were leaving Bajo Relibo on Day Fourteen, late of course, about ten o'clock, Cappy said he had something to say: "Four of the boys said they won't carry such heavy loads, and that's that." From right here, these four could still hike back two days to Truluka, but where we were going next, into the jungle heart of Costa Rica, there was no exit. So they were stating their position now.

Orlando offered more money.

They said no.

Elieser then said quietly that for his own reasons he was leaving the expedition, no matter what. This saddened me.

He was one of the kindest, certainly the most cheerful, and a helpful friend on the trail. I felt he shouldn't leave, but he seemed determined. Orlando paid him his salary, he picked up his walking stick, and swiftly walked into the jungle in the direction of Truluka, without looking back. Brett and I sadly watched him hike up the hill then disappear into the greenery. "Oh well," I sighed, "whatever he does in life, he'll be okay."

"He's not going to leave," Brett answered, and I wondered if he needed glasses.

"There's always one little rotten apple," said Orlando.

Then, for the millionth time, Orlando tried to get the loads lighter by arguing with Brett, who, under this new pressure, had no recourse but to FINALLY cooperate.

As an ax here and a shirt there were cast aside, Elieser was suddenly in our midst again, holding a handkerchief to his eyes. "He couldn't leave us," Cappy explained to my questioning look.

"Why?" I asked in Spanish. "He loves us too much?"

"Yes," said Cappy.

"Told ya," Brett smiled.

"See, Orlando," I said, "he's a good little apple after all."

"We don't know who's good until the end of the trip," Orlando answered.

"Well, I'm very glad he's back."

"Tell him," said Orlando. "Say '*Yo siento muy contenta.*'" So I told Elieser and gave him a hug.

Still with loads way too heavy, we staggered off. There were about eighteen in our group today plus two or three helpers from Federico's family—including his daughter who carried her one-month-old baby as well as a huge load. The baby was wrapped in cloth across her chest, nursing intermittently. Federico, who had now become one of us, would be our guide to San Locandi.

After only about an hour and a half, mostly walking on stepping stones along the river where it wasn't deep, we stopped. It was time to cross over then find the way on the other side. This fording location looked no different than other places we'd crossed, but now everyone put down their loads and Brett produced, from one of the huge bags, a rubber boat. I'd heard this boat was with us somewhere, and had hoped not to see it. I was certain we could get across this river on foot. Federico, too, indicated it was do-able, though it might have meant scouting for a shallower spot. The kind of men we had here would have enjoyed finding a way. But, as equipment master, this was Brett's moment. We'd been lugging this boat around for two weeks now—better find a use for it.

So we lost another hour taking turns blowing air into the rubber vessel as black clouds piled up over the sun. Choosing a rock for a loading pier, Brett then made seven or eight excursions across the rushing water. He was superb at shuttling us all across, and it was great fun, but the rain started before even the first crossing. And by the time the whole platoon was on the opposite bank, it was pouring horrendously and the river rapidly rising where we were beached. Plus another river fed into this one right here in front of us, and it, too, was rising. Behind the stony, ten-foot-wide beach was solid jungle and no trail. It was four p.m. and would be dark by five-thirty. We were supposed to be halfway to San Locandi and instead had barely started.

Temperaments were in poor shape. The men were still overloaded and resentful, and the loss of another day left everyone restless with unspent hiking energy. The differences between Brett and Orlando were grating on everyone. Brett was extremely slow, Orlando extremely fast; Brett wanted to discuss and communicate constantly, Orlando never; Brett wanted ample first-world comforts transported by third-world helpers, Orlando just wanted to keep moving so he could afford this out-of-control road show. When confronting each other, neither would yield, because Orlando was fiery and Brett a spoiled child. Brett resented being rushed or questioned, and Orlando never let up. So, because no one could walk away (Elieser had proven that), the clashes had become more and more intense and drawn out.

Now we were soaked through, the rain was crashing down, and we still had to crush the boat to get the air out in order to fold it back into its pack. The only thing to do was cut into the jungle right here, ten feet from the river, and penetrate deep enough to make a camp. So we did. But everything was filthy now, everyone cold, and we all just felt physically and mentally stuck.

The few conversations about the route ahead were in Spanish. I was pretty blindly trusting Orlando at this point, but Brett and Stacy were starting to ask questions similar to the ones I'd had way back in Punta del Sol. They were losing faith, but their alternative suggestions were anything but an improvement. Orlando and I now sat in our liquid tent as Carmela cooked outside under a plastic drop-cloth shelter the boys had constructed for her. Tensions were so high, something had to give. "There's a bottle of whiskey somewhere," I winked at Orlando. "Let's invite Stacy and Brett over for a little hoot."

"GREAT idea," he said, up for anything to restore unity in the camp. "Uh...Brett?" he spoke without volume because despite the downpour and seeming solitude, Stacy and Brett in their tent were actually about five feet from where we were, "Is there some whiskey somewhere?"

"There's a bottle of Canadian Club somewhere," Brett sounded amused. "Do you want me to pour some into a couple of glasses?"

"No," I piped in, "just bring over the whole bottle and have a drink with us."

"We can't," they laughed, "we're naked."

"That's okay," I winked at Orlando again, "so are we."

Stacy and Brett, now wearing shorts, were in our tent in about sixty seconds, bearing the unopened bottle. Having a toast together and forgetting the rain for a while was very, very good.

But it was my swan-song.

After nothing but rice, beans, and spaghetti, any new consumption now was so welcome that I forgot what I was dealing with. I figured the alcohol would help me fall asleep faster. (With the prospect of wet clothing and a wet sleeping bag, I was dreading the night ahead.) But I got rip-roaring drunk. Tonight, too, I had eaten a mound of Carmela's rice, cooked with pork. (Under these grim circumstances, it would be plain cruel to ask Carmela to cook something separate for me.) But having not eaten meat till now, it tasted foul indeed.

And the rest is somewhat patchy.

I just know that late that night, I was overcome with insecurity. I had expected to feel alone out here, but now I didn't feel safe anymore. I felt…unattended. From the deepest part of my gut, from a lower place than I could remember ever getting emotion from—past the heart and even the soul—this desperation came from my core. Now we were going into the jungle deeper still, and…I was afraid. Not in a wimpy way but in a life or death way. If I stayed with this expedition, I might not come through. Listening to two men arguing today for an hour or two as the river rose at our feet or as the boys prepared to abandon us (even though clearly no one could walk out of this)…was too crazy.

But where could I get away to? I couldn't.

Tonight I just wanted someone to hold me until I was warm again. I didn't want to lie in the wet tent, chilled and forlorn, with Orlando and Carmela beside me just as uncertain.

I only remember the most quaking despair, unleashed by whiskey.

So I fell apart, and cried. And finally, in the middle of the night, in the monsoon rains, I crawled out of the tent and across the wet, black jungle floor. I was LEAVING this expedition! On all fours. There must be a way out somehow.

I wanted Ernesto and Gregorio to help me, to comfort me, to acknowledge that maybe this kind of thing was harder for a woman (though it probably was the same for everyone). I even went next door to their tent. But they, and too many others for the size of the tent (including the woman and her baby), were asleep. Orlando came out into the black rain and tried to rescue me, but I flailed at his strong-armed attempts to subdue my madness, so he gave up. Brett then came out, found me crawling along, and led me back to my soggy sleeping bag. But that was just NOT where I wanted to go. I wanted something to happen—I wanted Ernesto to rescue me. I was wet and shivering and my sleeping bag was wetter still. But Brett put his big warm arm around me and steered me back, telling me that my plan to leave was completely off the wall.

Of course I knew this, but I was trying to force some kind of a change…my body just wasn't big enough to encompass the waves of despair coursing through it. I then gave up and left myself in the hands of whoever could handle me better than I could. And Brett turned out to be that person. He was kind and understanding and didn't seem disgusted with my inebriation. He tucked me back into my bag, and when he was assured I'd be alright, patted my head and went back to his own drenched tent.

But the instant he left, I crawled back out into the teaming rain—the situation couldn't possibly worsen, so I had nothing to lose. With both hands in front of me, I tried to feel for the trail, where we'd hacked our way in earlier. This time Carmela came after me and dragged me back. She was very firm, putting it to me straight that my behavior was *unacceptable*. But at the same time, she seemed to acknowledge the fear that prompted all this, and she guided my blurred anguish back to my sleeping bag. "We *have* to sleep," she told me, almost as a plea, and only then did I realize that everyone was sacrificing precious sleep due to my shenanigans.

DAY FIFTEEN I WOKE FROM A BLACK HOLE. I looked around to discover I'd actually vomited IN THE TENT. I turned to Carmela who was watching my arousal with some concern. Throughout the morning I had to avoid looking at anyone—God only knew what I said last night and who heard it. Meanwhile, I silently scrubbed out the tent and apologized to Carmela, Orlando, Brett, and Stacy. Orlando was generally disgusted. Carmela was worried about me. And Stacy and Brett said they'd been well entertained and my off-the-charts emotion had made them both feel better about their own. "I have broad shoulders," said Brett, "you should use them to lean on."

"I do," Stacy nodded, "all the time. But they're big enough for two."

But I still harbored the woe that had brought the whole thing on. I decided it was loneliness, and if the need to be personally cared for was important enough that I'd behave so inexcusably, then I better start finding a way out of this endless and convoluted adventure.

Orlando was still bent on going to Cielo Grande from San Locandi. At the rate we'd spent the first two weeks, this next leg could easily take a month. And everyone here seemed to possess a greater capacity for hardship than me. Even Carmela, though slower on the trail and more of a grumbler, had grown up eating nails.

I was totally humiliated today in front of Ernesto and Gregorio because Carmela told me they'd heard me in the night. So I kept to myself, thought hard, and endured another stupid morning of male jive confrontations as the clear weather stormed over again.

Washing out socks by the river, I saw the woman with the baby walking down the stony bank toward where we'd crossed the previous day. Being not only a woman but the mother of an infant, I wondered if she was having the same thoughts as me…that this was too rough. I watched her walking off. She seemed to be determining the prospects of going back instead of going ahead. Soon she returned and said something hurriedly to her father, Federico. Then she grabbed her stuff and went back down to the bank where she'd gone before. This was my chance to do the same, and I rushed over to prepare Orlando for what could be my swift exit. "I'm just going down the river a second to see what this Indian woman is going to do," I said hurriedly.

"You can't leave," said Orlando.

"If she can, I can."

"You do whatever you want." With steam issuing out his nostrils, he dismissed me and turned back to a conversation. After last night he probably figured I was a liability anyway. He knew the jungle would be the deciding factor ultimately.

I rushed off after the woman to see if she knew a place to get across the river without a boat, even though the river was now even higher than yesterday. If she crossed, I'd rush back, get my stuff, and follow her back to Federico's farm. From there, one way or another, I'd find my way back to Truluka. I could conceivably wait a while at Federico's for someone to pass through that I could then follow back to civilization. I had some money, and Chela was still there to act as translator for me. I'd be okay.

Someone was coming along about a hundred feet behind me. I turned to see Elieser. He gestured for me to stop, but I couldn't because I didn't want to lose sight of the Indian woman, and those Indians moved FAST. So he ran to catch up with me. He wanted to make sure I didn't do anything weird after my libations last night.

As we picked our way along the rocks together, I puffed out an explanation in mediocre Spanish, showing that I had some logic not just weakness and lack of courage. Since he was the one who'd tried leaving the previous day, he listened sympathetically to my reasoning.

Arriving at the bank where we'd crossed over the day before, we saw the woman just standing there, her baby tied across her breasts. She didn't move at all and we didn't know what her plan was. Meanwhile we knew the others were nearly ready to head out. I sat on a boulder in resignation and Elieser crouched in front of me and looked into my eyes. He was such a lovely person. "What's wrong?" he asked me. "Why do you want to leave?"

I thought about how to sum it up, and it came right down to one simple thing, that I didn't have the Spanish vocabulary for. So I told him in slow English, "My sleeping bag is wet."

He nodded in understanding, knowing as well as me that there was no way to dry it, and that sleepless nights would destroy you out here. He then took both my shoulders and said very carefully in Spanish, "You can sleep with me."

"I can?" I knew he meant it as a brother, and that simple offer was the human warmth that might make the difference.

"Yes." He took my hand and led me back to the camp.

Still not looking at anyone when we got back, I just put on my pack and stood by ready to go. We left at eleven o'clock, Brett generally displeased and inserting negative comments without realizing how draining it was to the group.

Day Fifteen gets the prize for worst day of the trip, if not my life. Expeditions and hangovers do not compromise with each other. You've just got two miserable ordeals to contend with simultaneously.

We started late and it was already raining. Drenched and filthy from the previous day, we all had heavier loads because all the clothing and tents were now soaked. (Plus there was the extra load the Indian woman had been carrying that had to be redistributed.) I was trying to keep my journal, paper, camera, lenses, and film from getting any wetter, but...most of this day was spent actually IN THE RIVER.

Our course was along the new river that had intersected the one we crossed yesterday. But there was no trail; we just crashed through the sopping jungle by the river's edge, under fallen trees, hauling ourselves up over huge boulders jutting halfway across the river, most of the time knee- or waist-deep in water, poking along with sticks or feeling with our boots to find safe treading under the water. And we had to weave back and forth across the river wherever it looked more realistic on the other side for pushing on through. All in the pelting rain. All day long. The river was chest-deep in places and twice I was nearly swept downstream by sweeping currents. Crossing these rapids, it took two men, with wooden poles bracing themselves, to help me. Alone, my weight was too light to stand up to the force of the water. All I was thinking about was the journal and camera. But I should've been thinking about my sleeping bag. Even though we all wore our yellow ponchos, there wasn't a dry morsel of anything on us or in the bags.

Today I realized how much communicating we did with our eyes. Being unable to look at anyone all day—due mainly to embarrassment but also to confusion about whether I could handle this, and how—left me completely isolated in my thoughts, and in the physical struggle. Without their eyes, I missed Ernesto, Elieser, Gregorio, Wilfredo, Cappy, and Wilbur, even though they were just up ahead or close behind. I felt like I'd walked out on them all by not looking at them, not sharing or connecting all day... but after last night I needed to somehow escape everyone the only way possible.

With my life at stake, and no one to turn to for moral support, I felt there really was no reason to look at anyone. I was alone in this and had to own up to it. In my hour of vulnerability last night, none of the guys had stepped out of their established roles to help me. So I had to conclude it was every man for himself, including women, and to dismiss any illusion of someone coming to my emotional rescue.

But I wasn't sure if I wanted total responsibility out here—I was the runt of the litter, the weak link; I'd probably be the first to succumb to the elements or get popped off...

This whole thing had become too dangerous. Today I had to figure out what course of action to take and how.

. . . . . .

We did not rest at all on Day Fifteen. We had a plate of spaghetti, beans, and plantain at seven a.m. and all the water we could drink throughout the day. We kept on moving, constantly on the grey river in the relentless rain, and none of us knew where we were going or how far that might be. Pushing through the great rushing river was so treacherous that Orlando became doubly concerned if anyone was out of sight. He was frantic all day, charging to the rear of the group about five times to holler for Brett and Stacy to hurry. Then he'd have to hurdle the rocks and rapids all over again to get back up front behind Federico. Supposedly (I learned later), we were trying to reach a certain place to cross the river a final time, then continue by land. With the rain not letting up, though, the river was rising, rising—and the day passing, passing. We HAD to speed up if we were to make that crossing.

Around four-thirty, we finally reached the spot where we were to cross—to an (invisible) trail on the other side. But the river was too high now. And the rapids everywhere along here rendered the boat useless. So Orlando and Brett blamed each other for the trouble while the rest of us sat on rocks, shivering in the rain as it grew dark. Three of the Indians had been ahead of us and apparently had already crossed the river, when it was lower, meaning we wouldn't see them again tonight. It was then ascertained that one of the three was carrying the pots and another the food. The Vanishing Cassike had again lived up to his name.

Every day we seemed to get closer to nowhere. We trusted these guides and often used actual trails, but these Indians constantly contradicted themselves—one minute it was two hours to the next river, later on they'd say it was five.

Following Frisky Federico now, still nimble as though it was a sunny morning in a meadow, we climbed up a muddy incline into the jungle to make camp in the rain. By some angelical fluke, Orlando remembered he'd haphazardly thrown one pot and three bags of spaghetti into a different bag that we actually had with us. We'd eat.

There was a definite tidal-wave-survivor atmosphere in our pitiful little gang as everyone summoned strength from the soles of their feet in order to erect shelters. Did anyone have a seedling of humor left? Not this drowned rat. "You know something," Brett approached me, "I've always wanted a waterfall right in my bedroom and here it is." He smiled and seemed to await my reply.

"Thanks for pointing out the positives, Brett. I hadn't seen it quite like that," was all I could muster. But I was genuinely impressed that he'd held onto some good stuff after the day we'd spent.

Adding to the disadvantages of the day, I was menstruating two weeks early. This partially explained the insecurity attack, but was otherwise unwelcome. All three women now, probably from over-exertion, had experienced this surprise, for which none of us was equipped. But fashion designer Stacy, ever creative, fabricated tampons from gauze and dental floss.

Like wet sock puppets on a clothesline, Carmela and I stood side by side under some broad leaves in the rain. In our dripping garb, we were silently updating our databases of despair. She was the only one who ever revealed emotions like mine when things became extreme—now, non-verbally, we shared a grim train of thought.

Fear, out here, had taken on an identity unlike any fear I could recall. It was so big, so present, yet a complete creation of the mind. I'd learned through this journey to dismiss it completely, to eject this impostor who tested one's courage or strength. But, depleted now, I had nothing inside except: How can I survive another day in the river if I don't get some sleep? Where will I get the energy I'll need for concentration? Why did I handicap myself with a hangover—I must be so dumb. What if things get worse still and we all fall apart, lose our way and our ability to reason? And worst of all, why am I succumbing to this horror?

I couldn't seem to neutralize my doubts in any way. I watched all the men struggling in the rain to make a clearing with machetes, then laboring to get the tents up, and wanted to help but was so rigid in my chilled angst that I couldn't move. My final effort went to protecting my spinal cord from the cold. There seemed to be an open window inside my back bone and the chill was coming from inside now, as if my blood was forty-five degrees. I knew physical activity would warm me, but my poncho lay covering my pack and without it in the rain I'd get wetter still... So I stayed half-sheltered under the wild banana trees with Carmela. I sent my mind to my spinal cord and surrounded it with warm protective thoughts. I could literally feel pneumonia leaning on my doorbell.

The tents, once the guys chopped jungle and got them up, had saturated floors. And when I retreated to my wet sleeping bag, as Carmela and Orlando miraculously commandeered the fire-building operation for the spaghetti, I knew the night ahead would be more miserable than I could bargain for. The inner chill was seeping in from all directions, in search of the slightest weakness of will (that was everywhere). Orlando, Brett, and everybody were equally demoralized—the life or death situation was here. One sick person, one fight, one limitation, and our progress would stop. We were days from anywhere, with too much cargo and almost no food. We were wet through and through, deflated, and the course was absurdly difficult—none of us had ever walked, much less hauled cargo, over guerrilla terrain like this.

For about three hours I lay in my wet sleeping bag, the cold ground against my bones. My hair was wet, as were my hands, feet, and clothing. I decided that, for me, this was survival time, though I'd never dreamed survival would be so emotional. Under circumstances like these, it seemed each person's needs and stamina were unique. Only I could determine what would help me, and then somehow secure it. Orlando, at this time, was difficult to endure, and mutual comfort would certainly not be found through him. I lay there knowing what I had to do, but wondering if such a simple thing was the solution. When nothing else came to mind, I elected to go with my impulse.

Warm bodies were the only answer to this night. And there was no way I'd snuggle up with Carmela, Orlando, Brett, or Stacy. Ernesto was off limits because if he'd wanted to help me through any of this he would have by now—though I did comprehend that, each in our own way, we were all on our knees.

So I went to seek out Elieser. I put on my sloshy boots in the dark, then slipped out of our tent and walked in the direction I'd seen him go. Elieser always camped with Cappy and Wilbur. Wherever they were, they were probably close together. They would understand. Most of the guys didn't have sleeping bags, just blankets that they spread over the plastic ground cloths.

Passing the tent of Gregorio, Wilfredo, and Ernesto, I popped my head inside to see what they were up to, as rain rolled off the rest of me. To my surprise, Cappy, Wilbur, and

Elieser were all bungled in there with them. They apparently hadn't the energy to build another shelter in the rain, nor the inclination to attempt sleep in a flooded lean-to. I balked at the sight of all six of them squished in there... How could I ask if there was room at THIS inn when clearly there was not? On the other hand, I had some more body heat to offer—though not much—and that was at a premium about now. A little novelty probably wouldn't hurt either at a time like this, and squeezing in with six men in a tent that uncomfortably slept five would at least be that.

"Hello," I ventured. "What's on TV?"

They actually seemed pleased at having a visitor—rare in these parts—and Ernesto flashed a happy smile, as he prepared his tiny territory for prostration. "Can I sleep here, too?" I asked the group at large, but looked to Elieser for the answer.

"Sure," they all said, "come on in!" There was a shared giggle as to what might happen with a woman smushed in there, but I also laughed because they were all so sweet. And I was so relieved that I didn't care if I slept standing up.

"My sleeping bag's wet," I said then. "Is it okay if I come in without one?"

"Sure," came the alto chorus.

"Okay, thanks. I'll be right back." I had to report back to Orlando, who might otherwise fear I'd rediscovered the Canadian Club and crawled back to Bajo Relibo. Of course what I was doing instead wouldn't bring a big smile either.

"Orlando?" I found him by the smoldering fire. "I'm going to sleep with the boys...it's warmer in their tent."

With the same resignation he'd displayed this morning, he threw his response like litter into a garbage can, "You do what you want." But I rejoiced at the ease of it. And Carmela would be the same with or without me in the other tent; but she'd never-ever-ever be party to actions like mine.

"Okay," I climbed into the boys' tent, leaving my muddy boots parked outside, "where should I sleep?" Everyone shrugged, looked at each other, and giggled again. I couldn't lie on the side perpendicular to them all because Wilfredo was already doing that, and I didn't have a blanket. So I'd have to squeeze in somewhere. Everyone was interested in what would happen. Elieser wanted me near, I knew, but he was edged against one wall; he would be my most compromising choice anyway. There was only one person I felt like nestling against, and that person was on the other end.

Suddenly Elieser said, "Ernesto, you decide where she should sleep." Ernesto looked around. There was about an inch between Gregorio and Wilbur, right in the middle. Gregorio put his hand there and asked Ernesto if that would be good. Ernesto didn't answer. So Gregorio patted the other side of his blanket, where there was no space at all, between himself and Ernesto. "Yes," said Ernesto, patting that space, as Gregorio moved over an eighth of an inch to make more room. "You sleep here," Ernesto instructed. Obediently I snuggled in, pleased to be beside him, and not too chagrined about Gregorio on my other side.

Elieser donated a blanket, and since Ernesto's was underneath us, I shared the humble donation with him, giving me an excuse to get close, though with seven in the tent, we couldn't have been much closer. Although I slept about fifteen minutes the whole night, the warmth and good feelings carried me all through the next day. Nothing at all transpired in the tent, we all just stayed close because it was so cold, like seven exhausted spoons, accidentally touching toes from time to time. No one slept soundly, needless to say, and whenever one person had to reposition or roll over, everyone else had to follow suit.

~ June 2, 1985 — the middle of nowhere — 3rd day on the way to San Locandi

DAY SIXTEEN

On Day Sixteen, we did not leap up at the crack of
dawn. Instead we just laid there, open-eyed, till about six,
all amazed Orlando hadn't come to roust us. At least the
rain had finally stopped.

I'd reached my limit though. At San Locandi, praise the
Lord we ever got there, I'd somehow boogie on back to
Spaceship Earth. This adventure had run its course as far
as my little soul was concerned. I didn't need to dally in this
life-or-death stuff for kicks. This crowd I'd been running with
these last few weeks was made of stronger mettle than me.
For a thirty-five-year-old *gringa* I was tough, but I was no
strapping twenty-one-year-old who felt well-employed under a hundred-pound load and knee-deep in a mud slide.
I was staggered by the strength of my new peer group.
These people had grown up around here. This rainy season didn't plague them, nor did being wet day in and out,
nor the heat of day, nor the jungle itself. They weren't left in
the dark by the language barrier, plus they were ambitious
young men dying for just this kind of challenge. (And they
were getting paid.) As ludicrous as the undertaking may be,
I had no doubts about their survival out there on any trail (or
absence of one) from San Locandi to Cielo Grande. But I
was no match for this mob.

I actually couldn't believe Orlando was still set on going all the way through. There were no inhabitants between
San Locandi and Cielo Grande—nothing but untouched
jungle. And San Locandi itself was an extremely remote
outpost consisting of three huts. To me it seemed like prac-
tically another whole expedition. Weren't we having enough
thrills and chills with this one?

It was so extreme to take twenty people and a bunch
of cargo through there in the rainy season, that I can't even

believe I'm writing this. I mean, six fantastically hardy natives, each carrying their own provisions and equipped to construct shelters each afternoon (before the rain started at about one-thirty and lasted till the next morning) could probably make it to Cielo Grande. It would realistically take six to eight days; and they would never get dry because they'd have to be walking, not drying clothes, while the sun was out in the mornings. Walking equalled sweating, so they'd just look and smell like wrecks, but so what? Taking twenty people and a chain saw and a rubber boat and a guitar, three gringos, God knew how many guns (that hadn't yet been needed), a bow and arrow (ditto), heavy iron cooking pots, water, three tents, and Brett's medical medley...possible maybe, but not for this fool.

If I had a man, right there with me emotionally, and to warm me at night, then sure, why not? But in the most desperate moments—and we'd now had some—I cringed at the sight of both Orlando and Brett. Not because they weren't good or right or strong...but because their spiritual connections with me, in both cases, were too hit or miss. Stacy and Carmela were my good, good buddies now, but they broke just as I did. It could get lonely out there and I feared I'd be invaded by pointlessness at the wrong impasse. The result could be pneumonia or a faulty step on a steep climb, a branch in my eye, the poison of a snake or plant (Brett had been bitten by a scorpion already—supposedly—and I'd seen six snakes so far, four deadly), or even a sprained ankle or too many infected cuts, bruises, and bites with only white rice and spaghetti left to rebuild strength. We rarely got much sleep and it was getting worse. Carmela was an ox, Ernesto a prince, Orlando a wizard—they'd all be fine. Brett and Stacy were so committed to this they could smell Cielo Grande from here, and the rest were young broncos. But what was I doing here?

Day Sixteen began with the customary shouting match between Orlando and Brett, followed by our weekly bible-reading since it was a Sunday. Sundays came by surprise and it was only the materialization of English and Spanish bibles from inside every bedroll that verified 'the holy day.' Cappy had one, Brett and Stacy had at least two, Orlando had one (claiming it was the only thing he was carrying that he wouldn't part with), and so did Ernesto. The little services were sweet though, with readings aloud in both tongues, and then the Lord's Prayer. It ended with the Costa Rican tradition of each person shaking hands with every other person. I stood back a bit and enjoyed it, and for the first time understood the meaning of "Forgive my trespasses as we forgive those who trespass against us." We were definitely trespassing on the Indians' land; they may not own it but only they knew it, used it, loved it. My own praise and thanks were less verbal than the others, but growing more poignant with each hour of each day.

We hit the trail around eleven, Orlando totally upset as always about the late start—the rest of us just tired. We did some heavy mud work, crossed some small arteries of the river, and after only about three hours of seriously overloaded hiking, came upon an irresistible clearing. Rarely did we find *ranchos* anymore, i.e. an existing structure to be used as shelter and often with some cleared land in the immediate vicinity. Here, too, we found The Vanishing Cassike and his cohorts waiting after their mischievous disappearance the night before with all the food. Orlando, once again, tried to impress upon them the importance of staying behind established leaders each day. This was hard for The Cassike to accept since he'd been our leader for the first days, but in these parts Federico was more familiar since his sister lived in San Locandi.

Here the sun shone down and a nice thatched roof covered the tiny hut. There was a stream, too. It was two-thirty and the clouds were gathering above. Waiting for Brett and Stacy to catch up, a half hour discussion took place in Spanish between The Cassike, Orlando, Federico, and his son, Rodrigo, about the path ahead. Apparently there wouldn't be any more streams for a while, to camp next to, and San Locandi couldn't possibly be reached till long after dark. (Orlando, fortunately for the rest of us, was alone in wanting to travel by flashlight.) So, early though it was, we camped here.

Federico told us a battle had been fought at this spot two hundred years ago and that one hundred men from one tribe had been found there, all killed by another tribe who'd attacked them while they were camping. This trail was two thousand years old, Federico said. (And hadn't been used since, by the looks of it.) The name of this place was Seekwaweeti. We all tried to pronounce it but couldn't, so Federico patiently said it over and over, "SEE-KWA-WEE-TI," until everyone could say it correctly. And 'Seekwaweeti' then became one of our buzzwords— someone would say it in the middle of nowhere and everyone would then rhythmically repeat it a few times.

Good thing we camped early because the rain came fast and, though still soaked from the days before, we at least had the tents up and some wood cut in time. Orlando, meanwhile, declared emphatically that, "Tomorrow we wake at four and leave at five." Right.

Cold and damp, I tried to dry my sleeping bag with body heat. At least we'd not been underwater all day, so things were better than the two previous nights. Carmela and Orlando were cooking up an incredible feast to make up for last night, adding the last two packs of some freeze-dried fricasseed chicken to our spaghetti (now that food had been retrieved from The Cassike), and whipping up rice and beans and plantain, and even popcorn for dessert. We could eat heartily tonight because when we got to San Locandi (tomorrow, no matter what), we'd get bananas, plantain, and chickens from the residents. And, also, Orlando and two or three boys would do a last-ditch food run to a 'village' seven hours from there.

I caught up on the journal by the weak light of one of the last dying flashlights. I thought again about my departure, my cold spine, and Orlando and Brett's ego clash, while Ernesto, barefoot in the rain, popped in and out of the tent, getting condiments and popcorn from the food bags. He was busy, I was remote. His tent was surely cozier than ours, but I was okay tonight.

We all went to bed early, drained in every sense. But my deep dream of huge jungle plants was suddenly interrupted by an urgent Orlando. "What time is it?" he was asking the darkness (i.e. me or Carmela).

Fumbling for the flashlight because my watch couldn't be read in the dark, I told him, without concealing my annoyance, "It's eleven-thirty."

"Oh," he said, dropping back down to his sleeping bag with a splash. And the next few hours were uneventful, except for Brett and Stacy vomiting all night next door. At ten to four, Orlando woke again, pranced around camp shouting, "Good morning!" and "Buenos dias!" at the locked and bolted tent flaps, then squirmed back in for morning prayer, that I do believe was actually uttered in a tone slightly lower than normal. (I'd been begging him to pray quieter.) At five, though, the fun was over; Carmela was raised, by Orlando, like a flag to fly from the coffee pot, and at five-thirty the Brett-Orlando roaring contest was underway.

❦

DAY SEVENTEEN

BRETT AND STACY WERE GREY AND FURIOUS on Day Seventeen. Truly sick all night, they expected some sympathy. Orlando was frenzied and maniacal, his mind squared on getting to San Locandi at any cost. We had no food, too much cargo, and a weary bedraggled band of diehards—all of whom had had major realizations these last days about the gravity of the undertaking. Like a ship too long at sea, we were looking for land—food, people, and a dry place to rest up.

But Brett and Stacy didn't feel up to the trip today. So a rather loud exchange took place when Orlando told them point blank that illness was out of the question right now. As Orlando and I arranged our packs in the tent, I quietly suggested that he give them some love and attention, that that's what they really wanted from him. Then a while later, I sneaked into their tent and reminded them not to take Orlando's antics as personal insults, that his hysteria was due to the pressure he was under to get everyone through this.

My tactics worked a little...Brett and Stacy stayed a good thirty minutes behind but at least made the trip. Brett couldn't manage his load though, so Orlando decided to once again leave some gear behind that a few people would go back for the following day—costing time, money, and manpower, all nearly extinct.

Aside from the river day, this trail was the vaguest we'd followed. At least half the day was slow-going because Federico and Rodrigo had to clear the way with machetes. Fortunately my load was lighter now. I loved the walking and climbing, and with a twenty-pound pack, could keep right up and enjoy the pilgrimage. Orlando made a gallant effort to keep heavy packs off the women, and though I felt painfully sorry for every single guy (except Brett, who carried less than the women), the fact was they could actually do it and we actually could not. Carmela no longer carried anything at all except her walking stick.

Everyone felt good about Day Seventeen. Mainly because even though we got up at four, we actually set out at seven-thirty. And going slowly made it much more pleasant. The hike was a pretty one because we went over two hills that afforded views. Ordinarily, even the peaks were too densely encased in canopy layers to see out. Today we were high, high up and looked out upon the surrounding green mountains we'd been crossing—though I'd lost my sense of direction on Day One. The white mist we'd seen from Alto Relibo was lingering between hills again and it was heavenly to behold so much untouched land, and to have come through it all on foot for seventeen days now. And to still be alive and alight and able to whisper, "*Que lindo*" (what beauty) to whoever was beside you.

In my case it was Ernesto, who I was content to be following again. His conscious way of stepping made easy following. He always pointed things out to me. Today it was one poisonous snake, a nutmeg tree, an anti-venom plant he'd shown me once before way back in the Punta del Sol jungle, and a huge ant-hill with black monsters well over an inch long (that Ernesto could smell beforehand). He also held occasional vines out of the way for me rather than just plunging through as we all more or less had to nearly all the time. I noticed, also, that as he moved a small twig or vine out of his way, he would bend it in the other direction to make it easier for me and those behind us. I learned to do that from walking with him, and later noticed Gregorio had picked up the courtesy, too.

Following the boots ahead, or picking out the steps yourself if no one was in front of you, was the gist of each day. It was always eyes down; but what a world down there. Bugs mostly. Leaves. Vines. Roots. Mud. Water. Stones. Tree trunks. Butterflies or flowers sporadically. Ferns, tendrils, webbed masses of lost vines. No litter ever. Nothing ever was seen that wasn't of the jungle.

After trekking about seven hours, we crossed one more stream, and things looked tamer on the opposite side. Climbing up, and still hacking our way through tunnels of undergrowth, we soon came upon an obvious neighborhood path, and then we passed banana and sugar cane growing. "Don't pick anything!" Orlando called back sternly (the temptation was great), after checking with Federico. "We'll buy what we need as soon as we get there." We then came to a small grove of very old bamboo growing thickly— the mature stalks fat and strong and encircled with green rings. Then, passing some cacao growing—the Indian cash crop here as well as in Relibo—we knew we were close.

The first hut was then spotted, nearly identical to those of Bajo and Alto Relibo. Two small children, home alone, cowered beside hammocks as we trooped over to a nearby tree and dropped our loads. These were the first people we'd seen in four days. The hut was Federico's sister's, so he soon reassured the children and learned that their parents were having a service with Padre Renaldo, who was "in town."

As the rain began, our group joined the kids in the mud-floored hut to wait for the adults. The little ones were impressed with our quick-change act as sudden raindrops triggered unanimous donning of the yellow ponchos…like bright butterflies spontaneously taking flight. The brilliant yellow looked fresh and punchy against the grey sheet of rain now dulling the piercing green jungle walls on all sides.

I went with Orlando and Federico to a neighboring hut up a hill so Orlando could buy food and possibly recruit workers to go with Rodrigo back to Seekwaweeti (SEE-KWA-WEE-TI) for the cargo we'd left in that *rancho*. We sat on a log outside in the rain, eating fabulous bananas Federico had been given, while Orlando translated for me what Federico had told him about the greeting ritual. "The custom is you sit and wait outside if nobody's home. (These people had also gone to see the Padre.) When they come back, they see you but they don't say anything. They see all of us sitting here when they arrive, but they ignore us completely. After they go inside, put down their loads or whatever, then they invite Federico in. Federico goes in and we stay outside. He greets them and talks a little, then he let us know when we can go in and meet them too. That the way they do it."

Sure enough, the people arrived and without words to even Federico, who was an old friend, walked right past us into the house. They moved around inside for a few moments then one came to the entrance. That stance was an invitational signal to Federico, who got up then and walked over. The greetings were surprisingly cool. In fact, everything about all the people up here was consistently reserved...the most reserved people I'd ever seen, in fact. After Federico was seated inside and drinking a cup of chicha, he nodded to Orlando. Only then could we enter, shake hands, and be acknowledged.

Right away I liked these folks. They were friendlier and warmer than the Alto Relibo tribe—maybe because Federico was a relative. (This particular family was related to Federico's sister and her husband, in the first hut.) The women and children had energy and smiles. In Alto Relibo they'd been sullen—though who wouldn't be with no food and no link to the rest of the world? Here in San Locandi, there were only three huts so it was an intimate place. Beautiful, too...cupped in a lush glade with a stream flowing through the middle, three small hills, each with a hut. These people looked healthier, too, and had light in their eyes.

In his inimitable fashion, Orlando put the whole community to work in a matter of moments. First he hired a woman and young boy to leave immediately with Rodrigo for Seekwaweeti. They ran off barefoot in the rain behind Rodrigo. Next he bought branches of bananas and plantain and four chickens. We then headed back down to the first hut, one of our boys carrying two chickens by the feet in each hand, and the rest of us laden with bananas and plantain.

The rain was coming down now and no one fancied pitching the tents in the downpour. Even the thought of rain made us all a little queasy. So everyone just lingered in the first hut with the two children, clinging to dryness for dear life. Fortunately there was a nice clearing right beside this hut, so if the adults consented to our staying there, at least hacking and clearing would be omitted. We waited for them inside, noshing orgiastically on bananas. Four or five in a row was standard fare at this point.

When the parents arrived, there was a brief consultation. Then Orlando came over to the rest of us with the best news we'd heard in days: there was an empty rancho just down the hill and across the stream, and we could use it for our camp. Jubilantly, we grabbed our packs and scooted down the mud bank in the rain, dashing like reindeer to keep contact with the rain as superficial as possible. The large hut we came to was an ideal sanctuary. Thatched, like the others, it would completely shelter us—and this one had an actual floor! Rickety but dry, the functional wood planks were about three and a half feet above the ground. (We'd find out later that another 'tribe' resided below it.) You could climb up into the *rancho* by either of two carved logs, one leaning against the back of the structure, one against the front. So we scrambled in, ecstatic about the protected spaciousness. All eighteen or so of us— depending on whether Federico and Rodrigo slept with us or with their relatives—could sprawl out nicely. And the floor was clean enough, by Karakima standards, to go barefoot. It was nirvana—happy, happy landings.

~ June 4, 1985, San Locandi.
Wonderful rancho. Clothes dry. Indians hanging around with us as rain falls all afternoon and evening. Waiting for Orlando, Ernesto, and co. to return from Cepequai.

. . . . . .

Things had changed a lot. Stacy and I laughed about it together. So much privacy had, by necessity, been abandoned along the way. With the rain thrashing down, and dry clothing the hottest possible commodity, nobody was about to get wet just to take a pee. So Stacy and I would simply crouch over the edge of the floor of the hut, hanging off the side and hoping not to topple off backwards into the mud (and hog yard) below. When numerous males were present (always), we'd wear a poncho as covering. People like Brett, Orlando, Ernesto, Gregorio, and Wilfredo didn't count and were trusted to just avert their eyes. As I've said before, in such an intimate situation, the power of a glance or the simple motion of moving away from the flock was always for a reason. When privacy was required, it was granted; no one wanted to make things more difficult for anyone. Carmela, on the other hand, would have none of this pornography, and preferred to wait half a day or even longer for an opportunity of absolute seclusion. I couldn't believe the distance she was willing to travel to avoid observance, though there wasn't much she could do on the trail about her see-through wet T-shirts. Another month out here and she'd probably be a naturalist, but meanwhile whenever I went to the woods for more serious business, or up or downstream a ways to lather up, I always invited her. And she'd gratefully join me, relieved to have a sentry or bodyguard. But she'd wait all day rather than ever go alone.

Our diet had changed, too. Bananas and plantain seemed to satisfy one's every need. Carmela had told me, way back in Alto Relibo, that she'd picked eight bananas one day, four for her and four for me, but that I'd never appeared so she ate them all. "You ate eight bananas?!" I had been astonished.

"Ye-es," she beamed back, with satisfaction.

But in the course of the next day in San Locandi, I myself ate eleven. This is possible when bananas are everywhere and nothing else in anywhere. (Plantain, by the way, count as banana.) In a typical day around here you might have two fried plantain for breakfast. Mid-morning you might happen upon a banana tree and scarf two or three for a snack or they might be handed to you as a gift. Later in the day you might look around for some because you're hungry and lunch doesn't really exist. And by then you're up to eight or nine. For dinner you'd surely have boiled plantain or dried banana or sweet plantain. And later, when you were talking to someone about how good they all tasted, that person might just have some ripe bananas handy or some square bananas that you've never tried, so you eat another one. And the next day you do it all over again, *con gusto.*

Those square ones, that actually have five sides, really are yummy. And so are the little ripe fat ones. Sweet plantain, fried in slices, is one of the most fulfilling foods I've ever had by itself, and regular plantain mashed and then fried like a patty with salt is equally scrumptious.

~ June 5, 1985 — early morning, San Locandi
. . . . . .

As we staked out rectangular spaces for sleeping, we became aware of the other group settling in for the night too close for comfort. Residing downstairs was a thriving colony of hogs. "Now I know why the man so happy to rent the place to us," said Orlando.

"Hope you got a good deal," I answered, barely audible above the grunting and snorting beneath the floor.

"He said we'll talk about the price in the morning," Orlando laughed.

"An honest man," I said, as the pigs made earthquake noises, and the probability of sleeping became unlikely. "They're right under US," I complained to Orlando, and dragged my sleeping bag away from the roaring. The sounds rupturing from these porkers were unlike anything any of us had ever heard.

"Is anyone sleeping there?" I pointed to an empty space in the middle of the floor.

"Me," said Gregorio from one of the hammocks that came with this luxury lounge.

"How about there?" I pointed to the next patch of floor.

"That's Wilfredo's," said Ernesto, sitting in the other hammock, quietly watching the full moon, silver behind black banana tree silhouettes. "And then is my space. You can sleep next to me."

Ernesto soon joined me on the floor. His sleeping bag was still wet, so I opened mine like a blanket and we spread it across us. With the disgusting thunderstorm under the floor—the hogs moving around in horrendous indigestion— the night was long and memorable. Periodically there'd be an unprecedented flare-up of gargled, growly grunting followed by resigned laughter as our group endured another sleepless night.

Except Orlando, who had the enviable faculty of switching himself on and off like a...siren, and who in the middle of the night awoke, sat bolt upright, and asked the general public what time it was. Since, again, I couldn't see my watch in the dark, and the question, in English, was clearly addressed to me, I nudged Ernesto who said it was one thirty-five. "Okay, Everybody," Orlando proclaimed, "one more hour then we get up." Then he blanked out again. Another snicker rippled around the *rancho*, no one grasping why eighteen people should get up at two-thirty so four of them could leave...whenever.

Orlando had made a decision to go the next day to Cepequai, seven hours away, to score provisions for the Cielo Grande operation. Ernesto, Gregorio, Ebelio, and The Cassike would all go with him to carry back the food. With luck, Orlando would also bring back some new men to carry freight in the days to come.

I planned to go to Cepequai with the others and from there get a bus back to somewhere on the regular map of Costa Rica. At the risk of sounding like the world's worst traveler, I didn't know which direction Cepequai was in, nor which town I might be able to get to from there, since Cepequai was not on the map. I'd just heard a rumor that there was a bus from there. A little earlier, however, I had removed my socks to find open sores between my painful toes, from the constant wetness. It might be saner to rest a day and air the feet, before walking seven hours to Cepequai. Also a day off might allow my boots and socks to dry. I had no idea whether or not I could manage a trip like that alone (though no doubt Orlando would support me with helpers), but if I waited for Orlando and Ernesto to get back I could then ask them what to expect from the trail.

Basically I didn't know what the hell I was doing, but saw a little extra time available here to heal wounds and rest, and decided to grab it and stay calm.

Stay or go? Things looked pretty risky either way. I knew Orlando was capable of talking me into continuing with the expedition, or that a few niceties from Ernesto could work the same trick. A great part of me wanted to continue, see it through, have the full feast...but another part felt unsafe. Not an overly cautious person, I did value my life and health. Orlando, for some paternal reason, was passionate about everyone hanging in there till the end. But who knew, after Cielo Grande he might come up with yet a further destination.

That evening after everyone had settled into the floor, he tiptoed over to my new spot, as I'd expected he might, for one of his pep talks. I'd witnessed and overheard several of these in recent weeks, whenever someone's doubt became a plan to abandon the ranks. Quite a technique he had, his success rate high in luring doubters back into the fold. Now it was my turn and here he was whispering that out of the original four he'd brought from the States, I'd proven to be the only one really strong enough for the trip. I decided to use these few one-on-one moments to wedge my point of view into his Airean eccentricity. "Orlando, just let me tell you why I want to leave," I began, wondering if this whole jumping ship stunt was just my contrivance to test affiliations. Regardless, I wanted him to mull a few things over on his seven-hour walk tomorrow, and now he was stuck listening for a change. "First: to Cielo Grande, for this group, is an eight-day journey at least."

"No, four," he interjected sharply.

"Let me finish... I feel we should prepare for at least eight days, possibly longer, when we're buying the food. Also, I'm disturbed about the arguing every day and I think it's ruining things for everybody, not just me. Are you and Brett going to cross the mountains with this kind of tension?"

"No, we're not," he said quickly. "I don't think those two can make the journey. They are not strong enough. So I don't think they will be coming with us."

"Well, I just think we have enough to worry about without the shouting."

"I agree."

"But there's another thing: I'm not made of this Costa Rican stuff you all have. I really could die up there. I just don't feel safe; I don't have the resistance that you all have."

Orlando started laughing, "You think I bring back a dead sister-in-law? How do that look?"

"I'm serious."

"Look," he said, "I don't think you should come with us tomorrow to shopping. I going to think this thing through. You stay here and when we all ready to leave for Cielo Grande, you see what you want to do."

"Okay. My feet are too sore to go tomorrow anyway."

Meanwhile my sleeping situation was snugger than usual. The wood floor was considerably warmer than the wet ground we knew so well. "Are you leaving tomorrow?" Ernesto asked as he climbed in next to me.

"No, not tomorrow," I answered. Then, in the darkness, I told him in whispers some of my fears: Orlando said this last leg of the trip would take four days, but I was certain, from what I'd seen of our movement so far with all our junk, and from what I'd heard from Indians, that it would take at least eight, maybe longer. Would we have enough food? Could we even carry enough food? What about the differences between Orlando and Brett? Was there going to be shouting every morning? And would there be enough men to carry stuff or would I, too, end up with a load too heavy? Or would I have to leave things behind along the way because people could no longer manage the weight? Were any of my fears justified?

Yes, Ernesto said, they were all justified.

I continued. And what about the mountain range? After all we'd done so far, I'd heard we'd only gone as high as three thousand feet. This range was ten thousand. The trip could easily take two weeks or more. What about Stacy's and Brett's health? She now had a bladder infection that she said was worsening daily. Brett was throwing up every night and generally only carried his pack about half the time. His answer to everything was to slow down, where Orlando's was to speed up. Could these two men get to Cielo Grande together? "What about you?" I asked Ernesto. "How do you feel about it all?"

"I'm just going ahead," his voice sort of shrugged, indicating that he'd made a firm decision at the beginning.

And of course he should, I thought.

It was nice to sleep next to Ernesto again. Nice, too, to have Brett and Stacy under the same roof with the rest of us. And nicest of all was that it was now two-thirty and Orlando was out cold.

❧

DAY EIGHTEEN

AT SIX O'CLOCK ON DAY EIGHTEEN, the few that had slept at all awoke, then kept shushing each other to keep Orlando and the pigs asleep as long as possible. But Elieser had decided to really leave the expedition this time, with the Cepequai contingent. And he needed to make good time in order to catch the alleged bus, therefore he roused Orlando.

At seven-thirty, Orlando, Ernesto, Gregorio, Ebelio, The Cassike, and Elieser left. The rest of us immediately got busy washing clothes for hours in the stream, like soap fetishists, hoping maybe they'd dry before the midday rains.

While we were scrubbing, the lady from the second hut we'd visited (and who only had one eye) came down asking if we had anything to trade. Stacy and I had brought along little items for just that purpose, but had been about to ditch them in order to lighten our loads. Good timing for the lady and her daughter, who loved everything we had— jewelry Stacy had made, and odds and ends I had, like nail polish, toothbrushes, and seashells—genuine treasures here. In exchange, the lady had small hand-woven baskets and calabash shells to use as bowls and spoons. We were mutually delighted.

The Indians lingered after the trading session and others came with their children to see Doctor Brett, who put medication on a baby's open sores and on the knee of a little girl who'd been cut by a machete.

Later that morning, I was washing dishes in the stream and the one-eyed woman came walking through on her way home. She had an easy humorous way about her, a kind of irony I hadn't seen in the other Locandia women. Street-smart comes to mind. She stopped, ankle-deep in the water, and studied me with that eye clearly doing the work of two. "You're going to Cielo Grande, too?" she asked in Spanish. She was the first Indian woman we'd met who spoke any Spanish.

"Si," I answered. Suddenly now I was indicating what Ernesto had indicated to me: I'm just going, come what may, it's out of my hands.

And this woman was now me, wondering about the safety. The sun dashed golden flakes across the running stream and the woman stood in the water squinting at me. I hoped she'd stay and talk a while, but the jungle life was both too casual for that and too formal at the same time. Instead of lingering, she looked off in the direction of Cielo Grande, then back to me. She then put her forearm in the air with her hand extended toward the mountains we would be walking through. "*Solo Dio*," she said. ("Only God.") She looked at me again. I nodded. She nodded, then continued up the trail.

Carmela then fried us lots of plantain, and while the rain fell we all just stayed in the hut, with entire wardrobes hanging damp from the inside rafters. In the afternoon, Rodrigo and the woman and young boy returned from Seekwaweeti with the cargo. Stacy, Carmela, and I observed that the woman had not only gone round trip barefoot, but with a load easily three times heavier than any of us had yet carried. She was over forty, too. We couldn't imagine doing what she'd done.

Day Eighteen was a healing day for those of us who stayed in San Locandi. We took it slow, ate fried plantain at intervals, fussed with our clothing, and joked about Orlando. Brett and Stacy seemed to be recouping their spirits, and we all agreed that silence was the only safe response to Orlando's brashness. It was important to remind ourselves, and often, that it was Orlando who had single-handedly orchestrated this whole road show, and no matter how bad things got, thankfulness was still everyone's foremost sentiment.

It was quiet with half the clan away. Orlando had said they'd be back that night, but no one expected them. It was unlikely he could generate a following for doing the return trip by moonlight and with cargo.

That night, Carmela, champion that she was, stood in her outside hut under the pouring rain, laughing with Wilfredo and Cappy, and produced another banquet. Rice, beans, chicken (none for me), and *chocho*, an avocado-shaped vegetable with carrot-like texture and taste.

By eight-fifteen we were all fed and in bed. The hogs were appeased now because along with us had come lots of banana peels. The longest sleep I'd had in four days was jarred though by one continuous dream that we were sleeping on the jungle floor, in the rain, with only dead leaves for bedding. During the night, I would open my eyes, see the rain coming down all around because the hut had no walls, and fall back to sleep sure the dream was real. And I'd look toward the rise Orlando and Ernesto had disappeared over and watch for them. They didn't come, and in the dream it seemed they never would again, nor would the rest of us return from the remote journey to Cielo Grande. Though I woke up rested, the dream felt truer than the sleep.

DAY NINETEEN

BRETT, STACY, AND I COULDN'T BELIEVE that Day Nineteen was Day Nineteen. Where had all those days gone, and how many were ahead? Despite the conflicts, a strange contentedness held us...this nomadic little way of life wasn't such a bad one. Or maybe our contented acceptance of the circumstances came from the simple fact that to leave the jungle was more dangerous and difficult than to stay.

Day Nineteen was dreamy. Rest days were a different kind of meditation than the silent hiking. These homey hours were of friendship and sharing thoughts and 'hot commodities,' as I now called everything from soap to dry T-shirts to half a foot of rope. We had only inner resources left, and rice and beans. In fact, when Rodrigo had appeared that morning, wearing bright red jeans, I'd offered to trade him a pig and two plantains for them, they were so darned nice. He said he'd play me a song on the guitar for the same deal, and did, even though I couldn't live up to my end.

The rain began at twelve-thirty, but this time we were safely under the thatched roof in dry clothing. We wrote, napped, and pondered the days ahead and our curious leader. It was good to have detente again with Stacy and Brett, who were always more tranquil in Orlando's absence. Around one-thirty, just as we voted to wait no more and get on with the rice and beans, we heard Orlando's "*Hola!*" up the trail.

It was a primitive and romantic feeling to be home when a group came in from a day or two on the trail. And their trail was one we wouldn't walk so there were questions and mystery. Seeing them arrive, though, so un-Hollywood, unpretentious, simply strong, gorgeous, and beat...was something you ache for in the city. Orlando came first, with stories all over his face, and wet clothing; and he answered my eyes immediately by saying the others were close behind. I watched the rise for Ernesto as Orlando shared his joy at being home. And it really was a family, rewarding to return to, because we all spoke jungle now and ate up every word of what they'd come upon out there.

Everyone was surprised to see Sinon returning with Orlando. Sinon had started out with us from Truluka, but had developed a stomach virus and had turned back after only three days. Being Indian, though, and intimate with jungle passage, he'd been okay about heading back unaccompanied. Apparently he'd not only made it back, but had somehow rematerialized in Cepequai, and now, *voilà*, was in our midst again. In keeping with Orlando's admirable policy of staying positive, he'd snapped up Sinon, who he believed could serve as the consummate guide for our final leg, due to his rare distinction of having previously traveled *eleven times* between San Locandi and Cielo Grande. (This was splendid news.)

Ernesto and Gregorio were next to arrive, bearing loads of food in plastic burlap bags on their shoulders. They, too, were worn through but rekindled by our happy faces. I exchanged welcome eyes with Ernesto, impressed at how strain and duress only strengthened him. Obviously depleted, his face was smooth and calm, his smile wide and sweet. They climbed up into the hut and unloaded the provisions, that Ernesto assured me would last at least ten days. There were bags and bags of white flour, lard, powdered milk, cocoa, sardines, chop suey (of all things), white sugar, white rice, oatmeal (thank God), and batteries—nothing particularly palatable or nutritious, but those adverbs were history now. Apparently they'd nearly bought out the little store in Cepequai. Orlando said it was the best thing that ever happened to that shopkeeper, that when he'd asked them what they wanted, they'd answered, "Everything you have in the store," and that he'd probably retired the minute they left.

Orlando went on to tell us about the journey. It seems the 'bus' was just more unfounded hearsay, typical in these parts. So to leave from Cepequai meant to walk from there all the way back to Truluka. Great. Poor Elieser. The walk from here to Cepequai had been done in six hours, at full speed, without cargo. Then it had taken them nine hours to come back with all the food. There were two rivers to cross, one where there were horses that ferried your packs over for you, and the other was crossed by a handmade suspension bridge that held one person at a time and took ten minutes to walk over. Orlando said he wouldn't cross it again for fifty thousand dollars and that he was only able to make it by thinking of his baby son.

Fabulous. What now? Was Orlando trying to scare me into staying? The weariness that encircled his band of shoppers certainly lent credulity to his tales; they were too drained to even eat for two hours. I decided to get Ernesto's slant on it, then weigh the facts. Meanwhile Orlando declared he was going to relax for two hours before...FRENZY!

~ *June 5, 1985 — San Locandi, eighteen people in the big hut in the rain*

. . . . . .

We didn't have the frenzy though. Instead, after a snooze, and while the troops sorted supplies and prepped for dinner, Orlando took me aside. He now had a plan that he rationally relayed to me. Stacy and Brett couldn't make the trip, he said. Delays, illness, arguing, and overload were wearing everyone out. One way or another, we had to leave without them. His tactic would be to tell them he didn't think Stacy was strong enough and that she should go out via Cepequai (with helpers of course); and then, most certainly, Brett would choose to go with her. If I wanted to go with them, it was an option—and a native boy would stay with me at all times—but Orlando would prefer I continue to Cielo Grande.

He then asked Brett and Stacy, who were buried under sleeping bags, to join the two of us for a meeting. Under a dangling florescent flashlight, and interrupted every thirty seconds by questions from the guys about preparations or food, as well as by local Indians trying to barter this and that, Orlando then pitched to the couple what he called his 'proposal.'

After yet another night of vomiting and another day of diarrhea, Brett was subdued and weak. Stacy, needless to say, became instantly angry but tried to contain it. She shot me several rigid looks, tapping my sisterhood with her. I envied no one a showdown with Orlando. But I stayed quiet, concealing my alliance, this time with our leader. It was ironic that Stacy and Brett were fifty times easier to deal with than Orlando, yet in the raw reality I knew Orlando's hardline stance was based on more than a hunch.

Orlando wasn't one for long-winded dissertations justifying his viewpoints. We were expected to be as instinctual as he and simply know when he knew what he was talking about. As I'd come to see him more clearly, through these crazy days, I'd discovered his experience to be vast and his aptitude high in learning from it all.

Stacy and Brett, sweet as they were, still hadn't left America behind. It was clear to all of us now that Orlando's plan of ripping through the mountains in four days, five maximum, and Brett's desire to get well first and then find his way along with or without the group, were two different epics. My feeling was that all the sickness and excuses were Brett's refusal to follow Orlando's style of expeditioning. But Orlando was our leader, and he (certainly not Brett) had gotten us this far.

~ June 6, 1985 — en route, first day after leaving San Locandi

࿐

PART IV - LAST GASP

BRETT AND STACY DECIDED to see how they felt in the morning. Somewhere in their hearts they had to know Orlando was right... I still didn't know which way I'd go, had been having jungle nightmares the last two nights—probably due to the hogs revolting, or the revolting hogs, down below. I asked Ernesto about the trek to Cepequai and he rolled his eyes. "Do you think I could do it alone?" I asked, though less motivated now by the likely accompaniment of Brett and Stacy.

"No. Too many river."

"And what about the Cielo Grande trail? Have you heard anything more about this?"

"Tigers. Too much tigers," was all he said. Lying next to him, he handed me a piece of chocolate in the dark. Chocolate had been the big prize of the Cepequai mission and some of it had even lasted the hike home.

The Indians up here were wide-eyed at the amount of food we'd procured in Cepequai. That evening, as some of them gathered beside our rancho, for final treatments from Doctor Brett or just to watch us, I noticed the clever one-eyed lady casually relieve us of a new bar of soap. As much as I'd have liked her to have it, we had run out, and, boys being boys, they'd purchased only one bar in Cepequai. The woman was hiding it behind her back. No one else had seen her take it. I had to somehow retrieve it.

Digging in my pack, I pulled out a necklace I'd shown her earlier. Since all the women and girls wore assorted beads, I knew she could use this jewelry one way or another. I approached her with it, smiling. "I want you to have this," I said, and put it into her empty hand. She admired it and smiled back. Then, in an opposite movement, not un-like Tai Chi, I held out my empty hand toward the hand she was hiding. It seemed natural for her to hand me the soap, and she did. "Thank you," I said, still smiling, and walked away.

The food scene was getting a little strange. Short-ages had triggered a new reaction: greed. Within our own intimate tribe, this was disturbing—yet I even found myself eating a lot when I could, to store it up, and I was probably spending half the calories the men were. Days earlier, Orlando had reminded all of us more than once that one of the secrets of jungle survival was to eat little, and I'd noticed that when doing that, water became like food, and energy and endurance were super high. But now even Orlando had succumbed to second helpings of dishes whose featured ingredient was lard. Eating was a sport here, a social oc-casion, and a psychological crutch in case my nightmares came true. The products we scored in Cepequai would have put any health conscious American on an immediate fast, but that didn't deter anyone here. And Carmela had a magic wand or something that made everything delicious.

But aside from our nutritionless menu, a lot of the boys had also 'ordered' their own food from the guys that went shopping. So certain factions now had stashes and ate at whim. They didn't share it, and ate again when Carmela cooked meals. I was kind of a feather-weight non-contend-er compared to these brutes, and had preferred eating less anyway under these circumstances…but this dynamic seemed to spotlight the one facet of traveling through the jungle that one wanted to completely leave behind: fear. A fear of not getting enough to eat was permeating the group.

But my most real fear was the wetness, the idea of a long wet day followed by a wet sleeping bag. I dreamed of it again that night.

Due to wetness, fear, greed, hunger, exhaustion, uncertainty, and being over budget and out of time, Orlando reiterated emphatically that this final leg of the trip would be fast. Four days. Where before I might've preferred a more cautious pace, now I was right with him. In fact, in the jungle I found the speed safer and smarter—in danger you don't dally. That was the message we'd been trying to drive home to Brett. But Brett thought it was fearful to even consider danger.

❧

DAY TWENTY DAWNED GLORIOUSLY and felt righteous. Brett and Stacy stayed in their sleeping bags, Brett still sick, Stacy still fighting the bladder infection. It was clear they would recuperate here in San Locandi, then walk back out via Cepequai, then Truluka. From there, they'd catch a bus back to Punta del Sol, then to San Jose, the capitol. One young boy, who Orlando had recruited in Cepequai, would stay with them all the way back. And they'd also have some San Locandi Indians with them as far as necessary. We'd all meet again outside the jungle, God willing.

Since Brett and Stacy wouldn't be crossing to Cielo Grande, my misgivings were tremendously quelled. Without the excess weight, without the shouting, and without the dawdling and sickness, our chances of getting there wildly improved. I was now excited about completing the trip.

But attempting Cielo Grande with no first-aid kit at all would be the reverse extreme of our current situation. I would play doctor these last few days and, with Brett's co-operation, would have a modest little black bag. But when Brett casually handed me half a bottle of aspirin, a tiny vial of iodine, and a few band-aids, I couldn't conceal my amazement, or should I say amusement. I politely asked if I could have some…more stuff.

"That's all I have," he answered flatly, with Stacy standing two inches behind him.

"C'mon, Brett," I had to smile, "you've got that whole huge case full of things." He rummaged around the many little boxes, as though none of it could possibly satisfy my request. "Can I have some gauze at least, in case somebody's really bleeding? You've certainly got gauze in there."

"Here." With questionable munificence he handed me a roll of it.

"And don't you have any ointment for bites?"

After more digging, he tossed me a half-used tube of something.

"Brett?"

"Yeah?"

"Don't you think we should be equipped for an emergency? I mean, what if someone breaks their arm? I know you have supplies for these things. Why have we been lugging this enormous case around if there's nothing in it?"

Brett was getting agitated. "You wouldn't know how to use most of this stuff—I mean I doubt you want the stethoscope or blood pressure equipment. That's what's in here."

I shook my head in frustration, peering into his case and seeing nothing but paramedic chaos. I'd expected to be given cotton, tape, ace bandages, an assortment of band-aids, maybe some scissors, tweezers, plain old emergency supplies. "Okay," I was giving up, "can I please have some more band-aids for everybody's toes?" (150 toes to be exact.)

He handed me eight more band-aids.

Luckily I had scissors, tape, band-aids, and even some gauze of my own to supplement this meager serving, but didn't feign pleasure as I knotted the tiny plastic bag, our entire new medical arsenal. "I think it's ludicrous for fifteen people to be setting out in this jungle with nothing for an emergency."

"You're the one who's always said we've had too much stuff," Brett replied.

"Brett, there's a difference. I can fit this in my pocket." Standing up to get on with my other preparations, I was comforted by thoughts of Ernesto and Orlando, who certainly would figure out common-sense methods of dealing with injuries. My next consolation was the presence of Federico, The Cassike, and Sinon—all Locandia Indians, surely privy to jungle remedies. Lastly, I looked to my own truest convictions, that real healing has little to do with the amount of Johnson and Johnson on hand, and injury doesn't occur in relation to how medically equipped one is. We'd been with God so far, and we'd stay with Him. The only occasions of illness to date had been Brett's and Stacy's, the ones ever challenged to find uses for their mobile hospital.

Fifteen of us set out at nine-thirty. Late, but it could've been worse. The sky was blue and we were finally on our way. We all knew, after twenty days together, that these fifteen—two women and thirteen men—were the right team for the last leg. This was the same group that had scooted down Aguila with the Indians. And the only *gringo* (*gringa*) was me. Whenever I'd heard or read about expeditions, jungle or otherwise, where there was one Westerner and the rest natives, I'd always wondered how that one non-native had managed to be part of it, or how one or two unattached women wound up marching along with a bunch of men. Now I knew: you wish and wish and wish, for years and years and years. Then suddenly one day, there you are.

Careening down the first mud slide, I was talking to myself hard and fast—working to keep control. We were going way out there now and already it felt different. We were flying, ankle deep in mud after just fifteen minutes—it might've even been quicksand but we were quicker.

We crossed two big rivers that day. The first we did on foot; it was only waist-deep and the rapids were manageable. Ernesto slipped at one point and started to slide away, but I was between him and the rocks and was being braced by two men, so he slid into us and was stopped. Being the smallest and lightest of the males, the rapids were harder on him.

The second river was deeper and we had to blow up the rubber boat again. Carmela and I wondered if these guys could pull it off—getting five loads across without Brett, who'd directed the feat last time. To our surprise, it was executed seamlessly and quicker than before. When I went across, with the last load since I'd been taking pictures, I had no qualms as we shot through the white water.

There would be no surety, though, until we took our packs off in Cielo Grande. And in Cepequai, Orlando had gotten wind of the same story Padre Renaldo had told Tomas and me that first day, about the gringos who set out from Cielo Grande to San Locandi not long ago—three men and one woman from Switzerland. On the last day before reaching San Locandi, the woman had fallen down a hill, broken bones, and died. Today we passed a huge tree with a date carved on the trunk: "29-3-85." March 29 of this year, just two and a half months ago. It had to have been carved by the Swiss men; this was where the woman died. The men had finished the journey—possibly carrying her body—and with all sense of achievement certainly obliterated by the tragedy.

Orlando kept this awareness close to heart; it was the impetus behind his endless pleading that we stay close together out here. (And yet we all knew by now that peace of mind came first, and should a person occasionally need detachment to attain that, it was probably a better risk.)

~ June 7, 1985 — morning in camp, 2nd day out from San Locandi

. . . . . .

Day Twenty was a lucky day. And we even pushed the luck a bit. Walking from nine-thirty to three-thirty, we didn't feel the first raindrops till three o'clock. But wanting to make serious distance to establish momentum, we hiked a little too long, and later, of course, had to endure the soaking, shivering routine under dripping leaves, our ponchos thrown over the baggage, as the men hacked clearings for the shelters. It was then Orlando disclosed that we only had one tent, explaining that he'd wanted to lighten the load. (We previously had three.)

There were fifteen of us... But some of the guys had been constructing tarpaulin-style shelters from the start, so that could continue. The rest of us would share the one tent.

With some pleading, Carmela and I got the boys to build the kitchen first so we had a tarp to stand under and hopefully the beginning of a fire for some warmth. But in the tropical jungle rains, there's no dry wood. Our chainsaw, that had broken back on Day Two, was now hauled out, as if wishing alone could revive its saturated soul. A new tribal ritual was being established—gathering each evening around the dead machine to coax and poke it with every conceivable object and incantation. Tonight, with our machete talent preoccupied thusly, darkness was falling, rain was falling, and hopes of getting dryer were falling. Without firewood, Carmela couldn't cook. Without the tent and tarps up, we all could only huddle in the downpour— chilled, exhausted, helpless, and irritable. Yet night after night, the men believed they'd restore the little D.O.A., and no reasoning could shake that faith.

In the end, of course, it came down to machetes.

Orlando was showing his unpleasant side this evening, so once he'd settled into the tent for the night, I stayed away. Tonight's kitchen was spacious, not too muddy, and had a chunky stone in it upon which I could sit, so I just hung with Carmela for hours and hours. The fire thawed our chilled sinews and the company was good. Ernesto, Gregorio, and Willy helped Carmela kill, skin, and cook one of the two chickens from San Locandi (I can't even write about the awfulness of this, but it's going on all over the planet every minute), then peeled onions and garlic, fetched water, and washed the rice. Carmela was at her best—being talked into making extra amounts, hot chocolate, anything to please us. Orlando was served in the tent, course after course, and never came out at all. (The rain did that to you—you were either in it or out of it.) This kitchen was the exception because you could be out of the rain but not confined to a tent.

The Old Man, as we now called Federico (who was 57), was sitting with us the entire evening and cut a poetic figure with his casual silence, watchful calm, and humble knowing. Both his face and his ways were innocent yet wise. For such a low profile, his was an elegant one. And he seemed unaware of his respected position with us. He still wouldn't hold your eyes for more than a second, keeping himself to himself, and just silently drying his shirt by the fire, holding it toward the flames on a stick, standing bare-waisted but never cold.

Federico was even more resilient than the others, if that was possible. He slept with no blanket at night, just became part of whatever he was lying on and was asleep in moments. I'd feel sorry for him if it wasn't such a waste of time. Envy made more sense. He wore the same torn and patched trousers every day with the same checkered polyester shirt, never buttoned, and black rubber boots. He had a rope for a belt—like lots of us at this point—and carried no personal effects whatsoever. Probably brushed his teeth with a twig and some mud. He could've given Siddhartha and Don Juan both a run for their money.

I was honored now to finally be exchanging greetings and words with him, remembering his earlier standoffishness that had lasted many days. I kept my communication minimal with him, though, preferring to let him feel invisible. He usually said nothing in camp, generally going unnoticed by all.

But on Night Twenty, The Old Man joined us in our sleeping tent. We numbered seven: Orlando, Carmela, The Old Man, Gregorio, Wilfredo, Ernesto, and myself. And what a night—Carmela thrashed around beside me, swearing about the conditions all night long. She was probably afraid to close her eyes with five men sleeping inches away. Space permitting nothing more comfortable, I slept on my side all night between Carmela's kicking and Ernesto's total tune-out. Looked like it would be the same role-call in the tent till the end, too, because the rain would continue… that was the one certainty.

❧

DAY TWENTY-ONE

WHEN I WOKE IN THE MORNING and folded the plastic we'd spread under the sleeping bags and blankets, I discovered I'd slept not on a nasty root or something in the ground as I'd assumed, but on a sack of rice coupled with a bag of powdered milk. (Another few weeks of this lifestyle and I'd be ready for a twig toothbrush.)

At ten to two on Day Twenty-One, Orlando was badly ignored when he tried to get things started. We rose at a tardy five instead. And even though Orlando decreed that there wasn't time to brew coffee, we didn't hit the trail till eight. Not so great for our plan of early starts, but after three sleepless hoggy nights, (and now no coffee), expeditioners were lagging.

Another sunny day, though…at a slower pace because we had a lot of cutting to do where vines obscured and consumed the path—when there was a path at all. Yet underneath everything, there did *seem* to be a skeletal trail dating way, way back. Following the feet of Orlando, Ernesto, or whoever was in front of me, we came upon no dwellings, no nothing, just jungle, rivers, brown leaves, and mud underfoot. Yet way out here, somehow, in this grand reserve of raw vegetation, was the faintest of paths that you could follow. But you almost had to smell it because it only existed sometimes, for certain people in certain moments… Sinon, with his laudable experience, now led the way; and to walk directly behind him was an adventure in itself. His confidence was staggering. I, personally, would never start hacking away at vines and trees if my trail was suddenly swallowed by foliage; I'd likely backtrack a ways to see where I went wrong. Not Sinon. Time after time he'd pierce the shrouding greenery, cutting tunnels through vegetation often for up to half an hour, then, to our astonishment, there would be the trail again snaking out the other side.

But even I had now developed a kind of jungle sense when no one was in front of me. I told Orlando, one of the first days out, that you could somehow tell which way someone had recently passed, and I described it as an orange glow, like heat, emanating from the ground in the direction the feet had passed. He had diplomatically replied that he didn't know about this phenomenon. But I had continued to follow that warmth left from human energy and found it to work. When I was alone, or in front of a small group, out of sight of those who'd gone ahead, I let the 'way' just pull me along.

Day Twenty-One was another gem. At eleven-thirty, after only three and a half hours climbing, and only one river crossing—I asked three different people how many rivers we'd crossed that day and only the third one was sure it was one and not two; days and rivers had become a watery blend—we came to the big mountain we'd been gearing up for. Sinon said it would be four hours up, then two hours down the other side. At its base, as we lay on hot boulders by a waterfall in the morning sun, Orlando asked the fourteen of us how we'd care to tackle this Alp.

Though too early to camp down here, camping at the summit didn't appeal because there'd be no streams, and we'd also be caught by rain before reaching the top. Going all the way up then down the other side was even more far-fetched. So we camped right where we were. Nice and early. We were wasted anyway.

When the rains came two hours later, our kitchen was up, fire burning, tent pitched, and clothes dry. What fluke logic had stricken Orlando before even twelve noon? No one knew, but all rejoiced in this sensible approach to handling the mountain.

Again that afternoon I sat in Carmela's kitchen. This time my seat was the canvas bag containing the rubber boat. The rain started at two-thirty. Orlando cat-napped in the adjacent tent, and beside the fire was the same group as the night before: The Old Man quietly watching as he slowly dried the clothes he was wearing by staying near the flames, Ernesto getting things Carmela asked for from the tent, Gregorio chopping garlic and plucking feathers from the second chicken whose head lay on a nearby heap of leaves, and Willy fetching water and filling in where needed. I wrote my journal on into the night by the fire's glow.

Carmela held court in the center—jolly, busy, and a wonder to all. Imagine cooking for fifteen or twenty people, twice a day for three weeks, on an open fire with nowhere to sit ninety-eight per cent of the time, smoke in your face and rain crashing down, no water except from the nearest creek or river, no accessories, and only two big pots and two rubber bowls, not to mention everybody's jeans and shirts hanging from the notches of the poles holding the rain cover, socks dangling from the makeshift cross-beams, and empty boots standing around the fires like dogs hoping for scraps. Also not to mention the poor chef had usually just hiked 4-7 hours through mountainous rain forest mush, and would be doing it again in the morning (after cooking breakfast), without enough sleep. I told her several times that of all the people on the expedition, she was the most amazing to me. She, more than anyone, had felt duped and misled in the beginning, had complained bitterly, and struggled with the hiking. Also she'd left her fourteen-year-old son at home with his grandmother, telling them (as Orlando had told her) that she'd be back in six days. And they hadn't heard from her since! Now she'd overcome it all and was right up with the front-runners during the day—strong as they come. She'd also lost about fifteen pounds, another testimonial to "The Orlando Diet," the sub-heading for my book, "Sweat and Fret."

What we had now, in this abridged version of our original club, was a sturdy mob. If anyone broke down or met with trouble, it wouldn't be theatrics anymore. These were people who wanted to make it through, who loved the adventure, who prayed we'd survive and well.

~ June 7, 1985 — Camping by the river, 2nd day after leaving San Locandi

. . . . . .

We ate supper in the tent that night, but Orlando was restless and uneasy so I went back out by the fire after eating. It was still early and Ernesto, Gregorio, and Wilfredo were trying to dry their socks, roasting them like marshmallows. "Wendy," Gregorio addressed me in his charming Pigeon English, "we want to go back to New York with you. All three of us."

"That would be fine," I laughed, "but I live in L.A."

"Okay, we come to L.A."

"I was thinking the same thing," I confessed. "It would be so much fun to stay together. We could really have a great time in L.A. I just wish I had a big house we could all live in, but my apartment's the size of that tent." Their enthusiastic faces fell.

"Really?" Ernesto looked at the puny tent in sad disbelief.

"Well, a little bigger, but not big enough for four of us. Why don't we all go to Punta del Sol instead and build a house for Ernesto?"

"Great! Okay!" They loved that idea. And we then discussed the ramifications of what we'd need, where we'd get a little money, and whether I should drive my VW bus down (through Guatemala, El Salvador, and Nicaragua—all at war) from L.A. It was lovely fantasizing together; the house was half built in ten minutes. Ernesto said he had excellent wood growing on his land and also a great river. The only thing missing was the money. He said it would take two thousand dollars to have the wood made suitable for the building.

"Couldn't we do it cheaper than that?" I asked, figuring I was probably sole bread-winner of the quartet.

"Maybe…" Ernesto mused. "I have a friend who might do it cheap."

I was surprised my new buddies were so gung-ho to hang out with me after the expedition and really wondered what their take on me was. Maybe they saw me as a big brother. Or a little brother. Fairy god-brother? Still, I was charmed.

The rain was falling only lightly and I moved away from them and the fire and stared out into the black jungle, listening to the river surging through. A smile crept across my face, there where no one could see me… Would we really build a house? I was touched by these bright young men, such fine people. Even their ambition and dreams were pure to me.

We slept badly again because without organization seven people really didn't fit in that tent. Orlando and 'organization' were strangers, and he was presently out cold smack in the middle. The entire food supply was now also stored in the tent, since things seemed to disappear otherwise—so we were human puzzle pieces that night.

Even without the vanishing rations, getting through these last days was a trial. Each person just hugged his or her inner strength, coping individually with circumstances, mud, rain, chill, and sleeplessness.

DAY TWENTY-TWO WAS HELL. Eye-rolls about Orlando's shouting were now commonplace. There were plenty of them as he blew off steam at Carmela over breakfast. Since everyone but me was on the payroll, the boys really couldn't take her side—probably for the best since there definitely would've been objection to his shouting at a woman. In addition, we were all dreading another Aguila as we prepared to scale Mount Boogo.

But Boogo was just not that bad. The climb actually started off as a piece of cake. However, Sinon seemed to have relayed the wrong data about what to expect from this day... We accomplished four hours up, plus a fifth hour not as steep, at which point we stopped to wait for stragglers. Once all had thumped in, Orlando produced two cans of sardines that we fifteen ravenously and gratefully shared. As we stood in the drizzle, watching the two cans being passed, everyone waiting hopefully for a second measly morsel, it struck me how hungry we'd become.

The rain had begun early, an hour before we reached the 'top.' The trouble started when we began our 'descent.' This descent was up. And up. And up. In fact, we never went down, even after walking another four and a half hours.

The rain was like every other day; but today, at ten thousand feet, as we turned south, staying at the 'summit,' and walked toward the place where the trail went west again (I assumed), it was *cold*. We got colder and wetter, and still never descended.

So we climbed and climbed, up and over, down a bit, then up higher. Finally reaching the ridge, the other side now rendered a change in vegetation—lots of moss, huge ferns, bamboo—a different jungle really—wetter, more flowers. It was a gorgeous transition—everything was new and different, but the thrill was diminished by a kind of chilly grudge against the whole mess. When every ligament and tendon is tightening around your bones and every muscle constricting around your innards to preserve that last patch of 98.6 deep in some Kundalini pit near your intestines, you don't goggle at the flora. We wished we could though, visual relief was better than no relief at all.

We were now in a muddy area, everyone hoping to stumble upon a river or stream so we could stop and camp. But the grimy little gorges we crossed never offered clean enough water, so on we bungled, noticing that the mud here was lighter in color, almost blond.

Orlando paused on the shallow bottom of one mud-bank, and I stopped short directly behind him. He bent for a handful of the light soil and examined it closely, straining some between his fingers. "There's copper, silver, and gold in this mud," he waved an arm toward the bronzed bank. "See? You can see it from here." Indeed, I could detect multi-hued glittering from the soil. Ernesto, behind me, had also scooped up a handful. He flecked through it, deciphering the silver, the copper, the gold, then closed his fingers around the soil, and held it up wistfully. "Two thousand dollars..." he smiled at me. We rubbed our hands off on our bemired pants and bent back into the trail. The pressure to get through fast was foremost in everyone's mind.

The marching was intense now. But another problem today was vines. They hung down from everything, chok-ing you by surprise. And black spaghetti coiled around your ankles. The Alto Relibo Scoot, that would've been a God-send here, wasn't safe—you had to take it slow. So, again, we were at war, everyone's face drained and sullen, courage reduced to a desperate need for a hot drink. We went on and on, believing we were going to descend and camp by a river at the bottom.

By four o'clock it was getting dark. Since three it had been clear we'd lost all chances of a dry camp, firewood, or the warmth of a lower altitude. But we needed clean water to camp beside, so we slogged on.

I finally approached Orlando with the suggestion to stop and camp anywhere we could, even without water, because feet were so sore, knees so pained, and everyone so depleted. He predictably scolded me for not trusting Sinon to do what had to be done, and said if we had to keep walking after dark we would. I reminded him that this wasn't the last day and we should preserve at least a little strength. I then retreated to the rear of the line where the attitude was calmer.

This walk was treacherous, but the extreme caution I'd used all day was so gripping that the tension made me colder. *I knew I absolutely had to relax my insides one way or another.* Finally, in sheer futility, I relinquished that concentrated struggle to keep finding more strength to push myself forward-up-over-and-through. I now became rubber instead, and just fell along, slipping, sliding…even singing. I simply had to relax. And this Raggedy Ann style of flop-footed trekking almost did me in a few times, as I stumped along. I'd step on a patch of leaves that had whole valleys concealed beneath them and my leg would suddenly disappear to the knee or thigh. But, still at an Olympic pace, all I could do was thank God I wasn't hurt and throw myself forward.

The Cassike, in front of me now, and probably worse off than me since he had more cargo, now glanced over his shoulder in disbelief at the sound of my little song. Following him, of course, was an additional hazard—it meant we both might vanish. And whenever those ahead of him were not seen for a spell, the thought definitely crossed my mind that we may not see the others till morning. Disappearing with a person like The Cassike would be an interesting interlude— I'd seen him smile maybe twice in twenty odd days. He had that Locandia reserve down to an art.

Today, in passing, he indicated with the tip of his machete a poisonous snake coiled in a spiral, just off the path. As I looked on, he hacked it to pieces then resumed the march. "What's the Spanish name of that snake?" I asked him, in Spanish, as I trotted along behind.

"What do you call it in English?" was his answer.

"*Touché*," I thought to myself (in French).

By now our hands were numb, my camera and journal soaked. I stopped Carmela and shared an orange I'd been saving for four days. These little treasures could lift spirits and energy when there was nothing else.

Then, glory be, we came to a creek in a gorgeous bamboo and palm glade, and . . . . . . stopped. It was four-thirty.

Carmela and I washed in the frigid stream while the kitchen was built. It then took at least two hours to chop wood, peeling away the outer bark with machetes in search of dry kindling. A fire was eventually smoldering, but not producing the heat we needed. Orlando retreated to the tent once it was up, so I kept company with Carmela again as she made hot oatmeal then spaghetti with tuna. Everyone was distressed that we were out of sugar. But I joyously gobbled two huge bowls of the unsweetened oatmeal that no one else could stomach, grateful for the nutrition.

Arriving late to the tent, four people were already prostrate—so it was catch as catch can. I caught the most uncomfortable spot I'd ever slept in, wedged in one rigid position against the soaking tent wall with rain puddling under me and dripping above. I had my usual dream about sleeping outside the tent in the rain, and got no comfort from Ernesto, next to me and just as squished. What made it all so delightful was knowing we had at least one more night of this and two more days. Probably more.

~ *June 9, 1985 — Palm glade camp — very cold and dreary*

THE LANGUAGE BARRIER kept hoards of information from me, so I always had to verify the weird info I caught wind of. The morning of Day Twenty-Three, I heard we were going to be in a lot of water.

"Is it true we're crossing thirty-eight rivers today?" I asked Ernesto, incredulously, expecting him to laugh and say something like, "No, four."

"Thirty-three," he answered.

Geographically, this just wasn't feasible, but something was afoot. I soon found out: we'd be crossing a few streams back and forth, wiggling-wiggling our way upstream. Fifteen feet outside of camp, our feet were already wet, though needless to say, the concept of 'dry' had been jettisoned weeks ago. I was off on the wrong wet foot anyway because Orlando had barked at me.

This getting up at four-thirty and leaving at nine-forty-five, though institutionalized now, was never comprehended. We'd be instructed at dawn to leap up and head on out, "no breakfast!"—always the military flare. Then Orlando would pray in the tent and everyone would get the fire started, mainly because there seemed to be plenty of time and Orlando would likely change his mind about food. Around five or six, he'd tell Carmela to make huge pots of rice or oatmeal or tortillas—taking another hour and a half...then eating...then cleaning up.

Everyone knew we'd suffer later for the late start, and have to keep marching rather than stopping early and camping, but...the mornings were kind of wonderful, our only time to putter and sort through unrecognizable heaps of molding brown clothing, determining which fetid pieces to put back on for today's hike. Thanks to plastic bags, the few battered ones we still clung to, I'd finally worked out a system of being gross by day—but so was everyone—and cleaner, dryer, and warmer at night. That is, cleaner, dryer, and warmer by Karakima standards, i.e. not at all clean but not muddy; damp and wet in patches, but not saturated. And 'warm'—thanks to the crowd in the tent—meant, actually pretty warm.

The novelty of being on an expedition, living in the jungle, being severed from the outer world, and doing everything as it was done hundreds of years ago, had worn thin. Now we all just wanted to get out—observe *some* signs of progress as we inched toward Cielo Grande. Day Twenty-Three was our fourth since San Locandi, and never seeing the sun hardly helped one's already obliterated sense of direction. Were we making any ground? The Indian paths traveled in snake-like ways and you could go around and around quite easily—it felt like we were doing just that.

When Brett had been with us, he'd referred to a compass at times like these and concluded that the Indians were giving us a run for our money since they were being paid by the day. Orlando saw no point in doubting them in their world. My limited experience of this terrain had me leaning toward the Indian method, too, rather than Brett's revered sporting goods. This wasn't the Kentucky woods. The determined Indians that first blazed this barely distinguishable trail did so instinctively with few clues to what lay ahead. And the absolute only way to cross a jungly mountain range would be to follow streams—up, up, up—rather than hacking through virgin rain forest according to directions from a compass. Following streams is easier, smarter, and faster. But doing so means winding in all directions as water has its own liquid logic to get where it's going. But, of course, if the stream does a one-eighty-degree turn then you abandon it, cut through the jungle, and hope to meet that same water again farther up. That's what we were now doing.

According to the ridiculously generalized 'map' I had, we'd follow the Rio Enok to the top of the mountain range (10,000 feet). From there, we'd continue without a river for a while, traveling slightly south. Later, we'd pick up the Rio Seebo for our descent to Cielo Grande. But we crossed so many streams today it seemed impossible they were all part of the Rio Enok. And what was more disconcerting was that all the water was running the opposite direction to our travel—i.e. down toward the Atlantic behind us. This could only mean that we hadn't reached the top of the mountains yet, because once we began our descent, the streams would have to flow the other way (west) toward the Pacific. According to my map, the top of the mountains marked the halfway point. If we weren't there yet, we had at least another four days. No one else seemed aware of this. (Not that we stopped for discussion. Ever.)

So Day Twenty-Three was again uphill. Apparently Mount Boogo was actually a series of mountains. The river we were looking for (Rio Seebo, I hoped), that we were supposed to have 'descended' down the previous day, didn't show up.

The day not only started off grueling, with me in tears from Orlando's abrasiveness—not lucid enough to grant him the same anxieties and jungle-fever we all had—but I continued to stumble along, nearly eliminating myself on loose nooses hanging above, hidden holes underfoot, and the torrents of the streams into which I tumbled four times. Halfway through the day, I figured this was it for me. So, sort of half-caring, I cracked open my last-ditch stash of sunflower seeds, preserved through everything, to be eaten if I ever found myself stranded, alone, and lost. That particular fear I no longer had; now I needed the sunflower seeds to distract my angry mind—truly the curse of the trail. But instead they stole my concentration, leaving me reckless.

Still I didn't care. Then my pack broke, and the camera and journal were nearly drowned in the spill.

I came to my senses then, realizing I HAD to collect myself and get some bearings. I engineered some space between the people in front and in back of me so I could wander alone. That was always soothing. The jungle was so strong and powerful, grand, and roaring in silence.

Once again, I was reassured and calmed by the beauty and peace of the Earth. This particular area we were traversing was rare and exquisite—Hollywood Tarzan stuff, moss-covered trees, perfect bird-song tranquility. I knew I hadn't taken nearly enough of the solace the jungle offers, and decided to enjoy the rest of the journey at a slower, more sensitive pace. I'd proven myself a trooper; I was able to hang in there up front, and I loved it; but now it might be ending and I wanted to somehow preserve this place in my soul. Only once in my lifetime would I do this—the most wondrous and rewarding experience I'd ever had.

I listened now for a voice that guides and helps me. It's harder to hear when others are around, but I was alone now and aware that my frame of mind was as muddy as the ground. Suddenly I heard the voice say, "No more rain." Even though the voice never lies, this news flash was too good to be true and I dared not believe it. But it was repeated, "No more rain. Don't worry."

Indeed, it was the worry about the rain (coming) that was debilitating—just knowing things would worsen rather than get easier as the day came to an end. Now the voice wanted to unburden me of the stress. Taking the advice, I relaxed my water-logged fear. I couldn't relay this happy dispatch to the others, nor reveal where it came from, but I later tried to ease their similar woes by saying I had a "feeling" it wasn't going to rain on us anymore.

And It didn't rain again for the rest of the trip.

    Carmela seemed to weave in and out of my day, keeping her own steady pace, so we chatted on the descents about what we'd eat when we got home. I'd have spinach pasta with garlic, butter, and grated cheese. I'd have a nice piece of grilled fish, five-grain pancakes with maple syrup, and a cheese omelette. Anything with butter and cheese. Carmela would have a cow-foot soup with onions, garlic, and *chocho*. She'd never heard of maple syrup, so knowing she loved sweets, I promised to send her some.

~ June 9, 1985

. . . . . .

    None of us now could seem to get enough of the silly foods we'd been scarfing out here. Powdered milk, with or without oatmeal, was guzzled hot or cold at any opportunity, and I couldn't wait to chug massive quantities of it when we got out. Bananas and plantain, no longer available, also topped my renovated list of necessities for life. I'd never again peel one without thinking of Bajo Relibo, or cook plantain without thoughts of Carmela.

    Yes, the food thing was out of hand. We had all become greedier. I fought it, but it was such a focus now, morning and evening. There was always enough and it consistently tasted better than those foods should, but second helpings were scarce and appetites ferocious. Unused to gobbling starch and sugar this way, I wondered where my control had gone. I didn't know it, but I'd lost fifteen pounds, and was, under the baggy glad-rags, a little skeleton. This unanimous gluttony was more justified than we realized; we were spending way more energy than we were replacing. But the exercise neutralized the otherwise ill effects one might expect from 'empty calories.' My system was so finely-tuned by now that sugar, white rice, spaghetti, and white flour slipped right down. The mind plays a mega role in health, too—if you really don't have a choice, you also don't have the guilt. So, physically, I felt fabulous—consuming two or three cups of hot chocolate at a sitting, even as a meal sometimes. Two huge glasses of coffee every morning. Mounds of white rice with lard, often twice a day. And nothing else. I never felt better!

On Day Twenty-Three we made camp late. Rio Seebo materialized *finally*, and we bungled through it to camp on the opposite bank. The kitchen tonight was small and deathly smoky, since the wood was so wet the stoking had to be continual. So I joined Orlando in the tent. Gregorio was already in there resting, after a slight fever the day before, and Willy and Ernesto were running errands back and forth from tent to kitchen.

When Orlando was relaxed, the camp was, and tonight was that way. After my sleeplessness the previous night, Orlando had said, "No one tell you you have sleep on the end. It's up to you to get enough space. You take space earlier tonight." So now I jumped in nice and early next to Gregorio. If Ernesto moved fast, he, too, might avoid being an end post.

Tonight I wanted to offer Ernesto something meaningful. A massage seemed apropos, so I instructed him to take off his shirt, saying he deserved this for carrying my bag over fourteen mountains.

Orlando looked on with a combination of surprise, indignation (I was mingling with the help again), amusement, and envy, as Ernesto obediently lay on his sleeping bag in his little gym shorts. I'd never touched him other than pulling the odd twig out of his hair, and felt it might be intrusive to suddenly probe around in his connective tissue. However, there was little else on the evening's agenda, and Ernesto (and all the guys) really needed this. "Legs first," I said, ignoring Orlando's loud thoughts. All of

152

us had major knee problems at this point, and hands-on treatment could only help.

Ernesto's muscles were so rock-solid I initially couldn't distinguish them from his bones. Even fully relaxed, warmed, oiled, and massaged, he retained an innate kind of animal strength. I wondered if the massage even made a difference to a cheetah like him, but certainly there was pleasure in it at least. But Ernesto still ended up on the end of the sleep line. And despite the sympathy we all had, the selflessness to trade places had gone the way of dry clothing.

At face value, seven in a small tent is comical. But with 'discomfort' as our theme, even humor wasn't funny anymore. The movement of a knee or elbow sent a ripple down the whole chain. Ernesto and I, on the end, at least had the freedom to shift our postures independently of the others, as long as we concurred. I would patiently wait for him to get uncomfortable, then when he stirred, I'd introduce a fresh position. Then Gregorio, on my other side, would gratefully follow suit.

❧

DAY TWENTY-FOUR

CARMELA AND I FIGURED another two days. Orlando, eternal optimist, wanted to push through today, Day Twenty-Four. "We leave immediately," he announced at five o'clock, bummed he'd overslept. "No breakfast, just cold milk." After twenty-three days of this, the boys were lighting the fire even as he spoke.

We were aiming to reach Las Palmas today, a village about twelve kilometers from Cielo Grande. Allegedly it would take seven hours minimum to get there. (Though it seemed to me we were still in the dead center of certifiable nowhere.) Sinon had been way off on some of his estimates, but I thought he might be right about this one because his mother lived in Las Palmas. Perhaps he recognized some landmarks or knew the distance from that upper ridge where the plants had changed. After eleven trips through here—though the place must transform rapidly and seasonally—he probably knew the last leg fairly well.

Seven hours climbing on an empty stomach would be madness though. Orlando somehow grasped this, and soon an enormous pot of rice was on the fire, flavored by our last onion and last can of tuna. And we had unsweetened coffee, thick with that Elixir of the Gods: powdered milk.

Around eight, we bit back into jungle warfare. The next two hours were a straight uphill mud-shoot—the grossest experience I could remember. We were calf-deep and climbing, and it was hard to believe this was now being served up after all we'd endured. "More and more" was truly the refrain out here—ever some brand new challenge. There is nothing like the jungle. In the wet season. We were nuts. This current situation was so hog-like that I was actually a little embarrassed. The plants seemed so much more elegant than us, so better equipped for this place. We were like determined little aliens, crawling along no matter what, in a place doing its utmost to reject us. We were microscopic parasites on some great creature that could snuff us with a twitch and was intending just that. (But it didn't rain.)

There were pleasant surprises, too. At the top was a broad view of the mountains we'd crossed: Karakima. And the ones ahead: Cordero. Could it be that the ones ahead were lower? There were the hanging clouds we'd seen the whole way shrouding the panorama, so we just breathed deep, gave thanks, and moved on down the trail.

More mud. Disgusting mud. Mud you'd never admit to your friends. Profane mud that made you hate the whole expedition and just want OUT. Two more hours of slippery, quagmire danger.

Going fast was impossible. We had to virtually unglue ourselves from every step. Before now we'd often gone through muddy places, but this was mud heaven; there was mud under the mud, mud next to the mud, mud after and before the mud. Then there was muddier mud and then even more mud, muddier than the muddier mud. We gushed through, never expecting to see our feet again. What made things particularly gruesome was that this mud was vertical. It's hard to climb up wet clay. These mud-shoots were without summits, and we could see only inches ahead due to the thick undergrowth. With all the slipping came sliding—that got mud on your clothes and pack, not that we much noticed—and grasping at things like vines, to stop the sliding. The whole endeavor was too primitive for comfort...to be literally crawling around in the mud. How long would this go on?

We ultimately reached a rise and heaved immense sighs of relief, only to discover that the downside, or downslide, was identical. And far too slippery for the Scoot. Just altogether vile. And that doesn't even tally in the exhaustion factor.

After the mud, I hung way, way back again, 'near' Carmela and The Old Man, who'd taken up the rear for this last leg—but keeping about a ten minute walk between them and myself. Since this was really the end, I was committed to spending my time quietly and slowly. Orlando now trusted my strength enough not to worry if he didn't see me.

With no one close ahead of me, I had to navigate for myself as the stream-crossing routine started again. I paused in the middle of one tributary, not seeing the path again on the other side and not knowing which way to search for it. So I waited for Federico. "*Ariba*," he said when he caught up, and held one forearm in the upstream direction. Nodding, I turned upstream, then re-established my solitude again. Continuing for another hour, crossing and re-crossing that and other streams eighteen times, I learned the Indian way. All eighteen times I found the trail again by turning upstream, "*ariba*." All by myself. Often it seemed the vague path could easily have resumed downstream from the crossing—there might have been a more accessible inlet back into the jungle there—but no. It re-commenced always upstream from where it had left us. And what an exquisite pleasure to navigate alone through this maze of winding water, climbing up waterfalls and across stones then back into the jungle for ten minutes, into another stream for ten or fifteen, then crossing three streams then back into the jungle. Up here, the stream was the trail, going up, always up, until you saw the path again. Wow.

It was fun, but cold. At the top, I heard the little voice again. This time it said, "No more mud." The rain prophecy had held accurate so far, and it had now been a day and a half, so I was elated by this latest bulletin.

~ *June 11, 1985*

. . . . . .

We came to another rise from whence we could see distant hillside fields. In both Alto Relibo and San Locandi this had indicated pasture or farmland. Too early for Las Palmas, where Sinon's mother lived, we still took it as an excellent indicator. A better sign was that the trail became a lilting fairy-tale path through a misty bamboo forest. Dead leaves and large red mushrooms with white polka-dots, of the Hansel and Gretel variety, decorated the way. No mud, rocks, tree-trunks, stumps, bogs, rivers, vines, thickets, tunnels, bridges, or Robin Hood fantasies.

There were more bugs here than usual but who cared? In fact, I was remembering all Brett's warnings in the begin-ning: "You'll have bites on your bites and blisters on your blis-ters; you'll have dirt and bugs in the creases of your elbows..." He'd gone on and on about how awful it would all feel, but he'd left out one thing: that we wouldn't care! Our minds had bigger fish to fry; negative thoughts were fatal.

When struggling up a mountain or trudging too many hours in the rain, one single negative thought could totally eclipse the razor focus needed to place your next step. Next thing you know you're down, annoyed, covered with mud, holding up the line, and you've still got to get up the mountain. So we'd disallow these, hopefully before a fall, but definitely after one. One or two faulty steps were sufficient warning to beware! your spirit was sinking.

The power of the mind wasn't just called upon in emer-gency, its work was full-time. It was also applied to overcom-ing drama within the group. And when the mind was at rest, we truly knew it—that's when we experienced the greatest glory of being here.

This primrose path through the bamboo glen went on and on. Hours, miles. I ambled silently along, assuming Or-lando and the rest were ahead and I'd not missed a turn-off somewhere; and knowing Carmela and The Old Man were not far behind. These sweet easy trails were so rare. Thanks came with every step, as well as apprehension about what might lie around the next bend.

~ June 11, 1985

. . . . . .

On one hand the big adventure was big enough now and the end would be welcome. On the other, I wanted to ramble forever, to just keep going, a Tolkien odyssey…to keep learning like this, the hard way. Going back to my L.A. apartment seemed tame, city life wimpy. Never before had I dropped out of contact for so long either. These last few days I could feel friends in L.A. seriously wondering if I was alright. Many didn't even know where I'd evaporated to. I'd said, "Adios for two weeks," and it would be six by the time I returned.

Whatever my next chapter might be, it seemed this experience should be a catalyst for a larger life—a truer and tougher one. I'd proven to myself something I'd known inside but had never really measured, that I was up to the job and could contend with nature and return elated.

But no one was singing victory yet. These last days were the scariest because until we walked out, OUT, of the jungle, alive and smiling, we hadn't made it. Orlando reminded us of this with every breath and move. The elements still had command and we…overwhelming humility.

From the bamboo lane I suddenly heard a distant hoot. It was Orlando letting me know the front-runners were waiting up ahead—maybe twenty minutes away. I hadn't seen them for hours, and sped up a little now, though cautiously.

Climbing up a rise leading to the field we'd seen earlier up in the distance, I saw the guys—dim silhouettes in a dense fog. And this field lent a spaciousness we'd not seen for days. Grabbing my camera I got a series of photos I knew would later show the expedition in all its poetry. The group harmony was visible in every movement, as they lifted their packs as one and fell into single file. We'd never founded any order or rules, yet all moved the same way now—fast, deliberate, strong, with equal space between each person. The motion was uniform, almost in step, all eyes downward on the path. But then something happened that made my camera limp in my hands.

As everyone trooped on across this fog-encased slope, with no hints as to what lay left, right, or ahead, only knowing we were atop a hill . . . . . . the fog far down below, at the base of the hill started to lift. And deep emerald canyons of the greenest, greenest, shimmering grass were revealed, the ridges glowing chartreuse in vaporized sunlight. The sight of non-jungle down there, in the direction we were headed, stopped us breathless in our tracks. We all just stood speechless and watched as, almost imperceptibly, the translucent fog curtain rose higher. The green valleys below grew bigger and wider and shinier. And what then beheld us, as the fog continued to rise—*timed perfectly for the precise moment of our arrival here*—was without exception the most breathtaking sight I've ever seen. All around us were being revealed the highest, greenest, widest hills in the universe. They embraced and encompassed us and filled the ground, the walls, and the sky. They went down, down—as far as we could look down, and they climbed up to the top of the sky—all glowing, shimmering green. And in front of us, they just rolled on and on forever, gently calling us downward. *We were out of the jungle.* The hill we were on was so extraordinarily high—above the green world, yet in it and just as green—and everything rippled and spread itself out in front and around our awestruck group of fifteen.

The fog then lifted even more, revealing beyond the green mountains rolling away before us, a green plain way off in the distance. And far beyond, we could see a town. It was Cielo Grande. Like Oz. And beyond that some blue hills. And those hills, we all knew, rolled down to the Pacific Ocean.

The whole magic show took only about fifteen minutes. And when the fog fully lifted, we could see about fifty miles and there was NO MORE JUNGLE.

No one had to tell us the expedition was over.

We looked slyly at each other and insuppressible smiles snuck out the corners of mouths hard-bitten by twenty-four days of rigid determination. We could see Cielo Grande and we knew we'd get there tonight.

But no one had told us about *this*—a sight worth everything we'd been through. A sight you'd do it all again for. And something clearly orchestrated for our little group at the precise moment of emergence from the jungle. "A symphony in motion," said Orlando.

Silently we picked up the pace and headed down into the greenness. I stayed behind in hallelujah bliss, carefully watching every stone as I descended the red dirt trail, and photographed the others disappearing over distant ridges. I was already cherishing the image forever and swimming in the one-time feeling of walking out of the jungle after twenty-four days.

It took at least an hour's delicate stepping to get down. I learned later that Orlando, Ernesto, Gregorio, Cappy, and Wilfredo had finished at a run. But after all these days, my feet suddenly wore out. Seeing the end allowed the body to collapse a little, where I couldn't have let it before. My toes now screamed in pain inside the mud-covered boots and socks that were black, full of gravel, and bunched up under my arches. Little bugs were chewing on my ankles, and suddenly each bug bite and sore was an open wound.

Down and down and down. I saw why the view had been so grand. We'd been on top of the whole world. And turning to look back to where we'd been, we saw a giant mountain, with other peaks behind it. A whole range, in fact.

The red trail down led to a river. When I finally got there, and fell to a stone to free my swollen feet from the fetid boots, Orlando was reading the bible under a tree and the others were bathed and calm-looking, intensity gone from faces.

But we still had more road ahead.

We packed up again and crossed the river, leaving a note on a tree for Carmela and The Old Man, still descending the green mountain. A mango tree was the next miraculous gift. No one has ever eaten mangos the way we scarfed those. Gregorio confessed later that he'd packed away fourteen, so

I wasn't as bashful about having inhaled a mere seven. The mango orgy was even halfheartedly repeated when we later happened upon another treeful. And even a third time at a small farm where the kindly owner offered us a basket load.

The trail eventually became a small dirt road and we came upon a few houses with thatched or tin roofs and men on horseback in cowboy hats and spurs. The people were as friendly as they were amazed to see such a parade from this unlikely direction.

Two men on horses said hi as they passed and asked about our travels. These locals were as shocked as the Locandia people had been that we'd done what we'd done. And I wished there was time to spend with them. If anyone could benefit from the information we now had about that trail, it was probably them. But we were sore and beat and it was getting late.

Suddenly one of the men on horseback told me that two days earlier a blonde woman in a Jeep had been on this road looking for a group of people that fit our description. "Did she have two babies?!" I asked.

"*Si.*"

Soon we came to the "store" that Sinon had told us about. This must be downtown Las Palmas. The shop was a tiny shack we emptied in minutes, cleaning out the already sparse shelves of every sardine, cookie, bottle of Sprite, can of tuna, and pack of powdered milk they had. After eating, we unpacked one of our huge iron pots and dumped in the last of our cocoa along with the powdered milk. Using the store counter as a kitchen table, we asked for some water and were obliged. Soon everyone, including half the town that had gathered for the spectacle, was drinking chocolate milk from our vat. "Orlando," I asked, "do you think we could say now that we made it?"

"I think now it's okay to say we made it," he answered. I hugged him and we raised our cups.

The men on horseback had told Orlando about the Darcy episode and he'd immediately coerced them into finding someone with a truck who would carry us the last few kilometers to Cielo Grande. There was no point in expeditioning along the paved road that began nearby. Besides, night was falling, feet were bleeding, mission accomplished, bellies full —and Orlando was DYING to see his wife and children. I, too, felt exceptionally fortunate to have a loved one at trail's end.

Ernesto now seemed like the very young man he was, laughing with his beautiful friends, Gregorio and Wilfredo. But I was still touched by the jungle man he also was, as well as the amazing man he would become. And I could thank him for his lovely face and helpful spirit that made the jungle easier for me.

. . . . . .

A small truck appeared with an open back and wooden railings. We overwhelmed the driver into taking all fifteen of us and the cargo. Our spirits were so high that if the truck failed us we'd simply fly the rest of the way. I scrambled in back with the boys, enjoying their cheerfulness for the final few miles. Orlando and Carmela rode in the cab with the driver. Seizing the moment, I asked Gregorio to thank everyone in Spanish for me, for helping me across the rivers, for carrying my stuff, and pitching the tents, for offering me food, and building the fires—for being so nice and for taking care of me so well.

Extremely jovial now that we were clearly in a VEHICLE and would walk NO MORE, everyone wore the biggest smiles I'd ever seen. Until we came to a flimsy homemade suspension bridge, not particularly short, swaying in the evening breeze. It had wooden tracks for the wheels to follow, so it was obviously built to accommodate cars, but this load? Far below (FAR below) were teaming rapids. We shared the thought of an ironic twist to an almost successful mission, and an exaggerated fear spread from face to face. The truck came to a stop at the entrance to the bridge, then delicately proceeded.

The old engine strained to get us across and the bridge sagged under the dire weight. We inched along, the truck rocking from side to side with no room for error. We looked back and forth at each other, suspended *way too high* above the flowing, rocky river below. Each holding our breath, and not daring to look down, it was still hard not to laugh. This was so in keeping with our daily fare, yet hardly what we expected right now. Plus we all might die in about 30 seconds.

We chugged along and got almost to the end of the straining little handmade bridge. Then the engine died. The truck stopped briefly, then began rolling backwards toward the middle of the bridge. No one could believe this was happening...

Reacting in unison, the boys reached over both sides to grasp the wires of the bridge, attempting to haul the weight of the truck along by pulling. But the engine caught again and we steamed forward once more, the tires gripping the wobbly wooden tracks and finally winning the last few feet of the swaying bridge. Then the engine gave out again. The outlandish overload was trying this poor truck as well as the poor bridge. We all sat captive in the back, some tugging at the wire cables. But after our recent activity, even this was just one more tough crossing. Stealing glances over the edge to the rapids far below, we were all probably most disturbed by the prospect of getting wet again. An invisible shrug rippled through the group as we half-prepared for the fall. Just another Karakima day.

Then the motor caught again. The driver, with more at stake perhaps, gave the accelerator all he had. All of us leaned into the forward motion, knowing this final thrust had to succeed. The truck grumbled sluggishly over the last wood plank and lumbered back onto the dirt road.

~ June 11, 1985 — Cielo Grande

CIELO GRANDE

THE GLIMMERING LIGHTS OF CIELO GRANDE were over a rise as we watched the mountains disappearing behind us. They looked so distant from here, so foreboding and mystical. The Atlantic side had been a gradual incline, so we'd never seen the whole awesome range squarely in front of us. The descent, though, was dramatically sudden. And once reaching the bottom, the cloud-covered peaks remained in our wake, hauntingly.

Truly they haunted and echoed, called, and even howled during our days in Cielo Grande. No one knew what to do about them though, the mountains. All the earthly power we'd felt from the jungle was emanating from those misty blue peaks against the eastern horizon. They looked so far away, and already... *felt* so far away. It seemed impossible we'd been enveloped in them, as in their womb, just earlier today...

Well, we made it. We did it. The obvious next thing would be to "dance all night and sleep all day," the celebration Gregorio and I had decided on over the campfire. A toast, a feast! We'd succeeded—at the most difficult thing any of us had ever attempted. But the gluttonous folly in the teeny Las Palmas store was the peak of our triumph. As in a race, a win can be rejoiced later over dinner, but the true victory is at the finish line.

In Cielo Grande the energy soon dispersed. Depositing us in barracks, just a step up from the Truluka Ritz, Orlando vanished in search of his family. According to half the tiny town, Darcy was lodged two blocks away with her kids, and had been for ten days—another endurance trial, judging from the proportions of this hamlet. Even in the first hours of hooking back into the outside world, we knew we were foreign here.

Orlando's idea of involving the family in something as mammoth as an expedition was a wise one. I was blessed to have Darcy around. She sought me out later that evening, after Orlando and the kids had collapsed, as anxious to hear the crazy tale as I was to tell it—or bits and pieces as I leapt around among jungle images answering her questions. It was wonderful to see her. She thanked me for the letter I'd sent out with Tomas, where I'd communicated our many delays, and told me she'd have really worried otherwise.

Carmela wasn't the only one who'd lost weight, Darcy informed me. And the looseness of the clothes she now lent me confirmed it. I'd thought my jungle attire had just become baggy from wetness and filth, but in the mirror I looked like a malnourished twelve-year-old boy. (Probably the only indication of my gender out there had been my tears.) I'd entered the jungle weighing maybe 124 pounds, and was now under 110.

But here in Cielo Grande we could all get down to some serious eating. We commenced our re-entry program the next morning with three breakfasts each. Yet all we ate that day, and the days that followed, filled only our stomachs, not our appetites. A curious hunger went on for not hours, not days, but weeks. Even our feet seemed insatiable. Feeding oneself was like feeding the whole gang—every ligament, every fingernail wanted some too, and then some more, please. On the positive side, as if eating like fiends wasn't enough fun, the muscles I'd developed were awesome. My skinny little back looked like the knitted pattern of a sweater.

So we all tended to our stomachs and our feet. Everyone had advanced Athlete's Foot—crusty bleeding between each and every toe, from all that moisture. Speaking little, everyone either hobbled along the narrow corridor of our hotel, or fussed with clothes-related activity in our cells. This dorm outranked the Truluka dive in having running water at least, but without warning it was shut off early each evening, usually before we'd showered. A la the 'Ritz,' this coop, too, was without windows, so by seven p.m. when the lights snapped on, we'd been waiting all day to get petty things accomplished. (Another reason to hang out in the restaurant.)

We only spent two days in Cielo Grande, but an insidious restlessness instantly invaded. Unpracticed with idleness, and with our metabolisms geared to overdrive, we were jumpy and unfulfilled, wanting to climb over everything.

Everyone in our tribe looked corny out here—clean and combed. Most of us had had to buy new clothes, too, so we found it tricky to relate as we had before, nobody looked like they should. Everything felt tried and slow, like that one day of the year when kids dress up for the class photograph. And, without all the activity we'd grown accustomed to, communication could only be verbal now. Yet the language barrier, among other things, prevented that. Federico was really out of his element now. His stature had noticeably diminished. In wearing his same clothes, he just didn't cut it as a city-slicker. None of us did; the jungle was so much more glamorous.

So as the afternoon rains flooded the streets, we just sat on the covered balcony or in the restaurant, nibbling on pastries and wondering what the plants were doing back in the jungle. A numbness prevailed; a post-natal depression maybe... What do we do now? Do we stride around in army clothes flexing our muscles? Do we return home and fill our rooms with tropical foliage? Relieved as we were to be done with the 'ordeal' of it, we were also thoroughly trained and capable now of just about anything—bring it on. To discard this phenomenal skill-set felt wasteful and frustrating. (Possibly what soldiers feel like coming home; their fine-tuned human instruments and honed skills will never be needed again, nor will they be side by side again with those who shared their struggle.)

Compared to recent weeks, L.A. offered nothing. To return there would be like going back to elementary school. Was there some way I could keep this ball rolling? (I was definitely game for building that jungle habitat on Ernesto's land.) But being back in society was making me a female again, and Carmela and I, stashed in our sauna-like chamber, would pass our male cohorts in the hall and have nothing to say. We were all caged animals, and words or meaningless smiles weren't going to alter the frustration. For everyone, it was an awkward and pensive time.

Meanwhile, all the guys were locked into fee negotiations with Orlando. Originally, each had made a personal deal with him as to how much per day. In the end, though, the work done was pretty equal. In fact, Gregorio and Wilfredo had signed on for less pay than the others, being the youngest, but had been ever-willing to do extra around camp for the duration of the trip. Right now, though—after all the overages and extra days—Orlando simply didn't have enough cash, so negotiation wasn't possible. His time was spent contacting his brother in San Jose, to arrange for money to be sent from New York. So everyone was stewing for one reason or another.

I sampled the town's cuisine between lazy musings with Carmela, Darcy, or both. Another question that popped up intermittently was, "What ever happened to Stacy and Brett?" We'd half-expected them to be with Darcy in Cielo Grande, but she'd heard nothing from them.

Like bunk-mates at some camp, Carmela and I were close now. Because she lived in Punta del Sol, like Ernesto, and had known him all her life, I'd never confided to her any sentiments about him. As we sat alone together in the restaurant the second evening, wondering what to order next, I wondered if she'd developed feelings for anyone on the expedition. She hadn't shown anything. "Carmela, if there was one person on the expedition that you felt something for more than any of the others, who would it be?"

With a twinkle, she answered, "Maybe Cappy..."

I was amazed; and relieved, too, that someone else had experienced the necessity to hold back. "Does he know?" I asked her.

"No-o-o. I don't show it."

"Why not?"

"Cappy don't care for me."

"How do you know?"

"I know. But I *likes* him. He's ni-i-ce." Carmela was blushing.

"You know who I liked?" I asked coyly.

"Ernesto," she said, matter-of-factly.

"How'd you know?"

"I see. I have h-eyes,"

"Do you think he knows?"

"I don't know. Maybe... He tell me something that last day in the jungle..."

"What?"

"He say, 'Carmela, was you cold last night?' And I say, 'Yes, I was co-old.' And he say, 'Well not me... Wendy keep me warm and I keep her warm.'"

"He told you that?"

"Ye-es."

"Well, nothing happened, but being close did keep us both warm. Anyway, he has a girlfriend back in Punta del Sol, doesn't he?"

"No," said Carmela.

"Yes, he must have a girl."

"No," she said firmly, "he have no girl."

"Well, I don't understand Costa Rican men."

"What you mean?"

"They don't do anything."

"What you mean?"

"Well, they don't show anything."

"Who you mean? Ernesto?"

"Yeah."

"He can't!"

"Why?"

"He have SHAME!"

"What do you mean?"

"He have shame—he ashamed!"

"I don't know what you mean. You mean shy?"

"He have shame, I tell you. We in Costa Rica, we have shame. That's the way we are," she said with pride.

(Humility, modesty, respect? Deference? Was this 'shame,' so obvious to Carmela, something we Americans don't even have a word for?) I was never to have it explained.

Orlando and I still had to put the finishing touches on the expedition. Even though he'd lost three-quarters of his gringos, he was still determined to end up IN the Pacific Ocean—that way we'd have truly crossed from Atlantic to Pacific. Few countries offer both coasts, and fewer still can be crossed on foot in a matter of weeks. We weren't going to walk to the beach, though, it was another thirty kilometers. We'd cut over to the shore in the Jeep on our drive back to San Jose. So the third morning, Carmela and all the guys took a six a.m. bus to San Jose. Their trip would take four hours. Orlando, Darcy, the children, and I would meet them there.

Our ceremonial Pacific swim was minimal, with only two members of the expedition present. But for Orlando and me it was a last cadence of accomplishment. And it was ironic that, out of the original USA contingent, only we two had completed his mission. Somewhere inside I'd envisioned it that way from the start, maybe because of the family connection, maybe personalities, who knows? I just never doubted Orlando's determination or ability, and despite my own weakness and misgivings, I was enthralled with the experience from Day One.

With our arms around each other, we stood before the ocean as Darcy snapped the official photo. It wasn't automatic for us to touch one another, after clashing so often, but we were in sync today—we both loved oceans and swimming and traveling and Darcy and eating (that we'd been doing non-stop since Las Palmas).

"I'd be concerned if it was just one of you eating like this," said Darcy, "but since you're both doing it, I'll just assume you're starving."

Orlando and I had to be a little careful in each other's company now—our bond was of respect and shared victory more than camaraderie or likeness. Still, I had a sneaky suspicion that if he ever, in a moment of forgetfulness, invited me on another expedition, I'd accept as eagerly as this time. Despite everything, I trusted his jungle instincts, his strength, prowess, drive, generosity, and unsurpassed courage.

THE REST OF THE GROUP had a surprise reception in San Jose. As they filed off the bus, they were promptly arrested and plunked into jail. Apparently somebody in Cielo Grande had viewed our activity with suspicion—a unidentified platoon emerging from the remote mountain jungles—and reported to the San Jose police that this group could only be Nicaraguan Sandinista soldiers. Pro-American Costa Rica didn't sympathize with the Sandinista struggle of Nicaragua, its northern neighbor, so paranoia about filthy guerrilla-types moving through the jungly mountains wasn't at all far-fetched. But although it took two and a half hours, Cappy's military credential, as well as probably everything else about this troop, overruled the accusation.

The money from New York was slow in coming, so we had another two days in San Jose. Since my return ticket to L.A. had expired, we'd tend to that shortly. Orlando had to get the men signed off first since they were still being paid by the day.

So Darcy and I cruised the markets or played by the pool with Maya and Marco. I saw little of Ernesto who, with Gregorio and Willy, was decompressing in his own way. Our common denominators were evaporating in this urban backdrop. And my sibling's presence linked me involuntarily to a sizable history elsewhere, not to mention age and race differences (none of the above pertinent to fanciful performance of the Alto Relibo Scoot). I was being sucked away from jungle memories, away from what I'd learned, away from the awake, agile being I'd become... sucked backwards to what I'd been before. It was all wrong.

Some of the money then came, and Cappy and most of the others left. Orlando had asked Ernesto, Gregorio, and Wilfredo to be patient until the rest of the cash arrived. The second afternoon, Darcy and I were sitting in the hotel restaurant, biding time like you do on a ship or train. At a nearby table, Ernesto, Gregorio, and Wilfredo appeared to be doing the same. Glancing in their direction, though, I noticed baggage beside them. And moments later, a taxi rolled up to the entrance. I turned again to see my three friends rising and picking up their luggage. Darcy and I walked with the children out into the driveway, where Orlando and Carmela had also appeared, to say goodbye to the boys.

Struck with confusion, it seemed incredible that Ernesto would now leave my life forever. Gregorio and Wilfredo sweetly said goodbye to me and got into the cab. Then I felt a hand touch my arm from the other side, and turned to see Ernesto. "Wendy..." he said, and kissed my cheek.

"Ernesto," I threw both arms around him and pressed my cheek against his warm neck. We then stood back from each other and both said goodbye. The cab was waiting so he turned and walked to it.

As he opened the car door, he wore an expression I hadn't seen before. Always he'd displayed that calm; in the face of everything, he'd projected that serene exterior. Now a little frown had appeared. His gaze was downward, his motion deliberate, but something wasn't right. The car door closed and the cab backed out of the drive. The windows were being rolled down and waving arms emerged as the taxi moved forward now. As Maya and I waved, I looked into the back window for Ernesto's face. He waved to me, the frown unchanged. And the car vanished.

I looked at Darcy and she looked at me. "Does he have your address?" she asked.

"No."

I asked little two-year-old Maya then if she'd like to walk by the pool with me and she readily agreed. As soon as we rounded the corner, I let the tears fall. Even though this was clearly the way it was meant to be, and it was okay, and I understood…still it was sad.

"Why are you crying, Aunt Wendy?" Maya had witnessed no cause for these tears.

"I guess I'm just a baby, Maya."

"I'm not a baby," she said, appeased momentarily. Then, "Why *are* you crying?" She was staring at me, trying to figure it out.

I looked at her through the tears, as her concern mounted. "I'm crying because I really like Ernesto, and now he left," I told her.

"Oh." She waited for more.

"And I might never see him again."

"Oh-h," she nodded sadly.

Carmela left that night. We agreed to write and I knew we would.

For the next day, Orlando, true to form, had arranged a couple of television interviews for Federico, who was still reeling from the novelty of staying in a hotel. I was to stand beside him, but got rejected at both TV stations because of my lousy Spanish, so the poor "Locandia Chief" had to wing it. He did beautifully in Orlando's white shirt and cowboy style tie. Federico handled his television debut with elegance, but I couldn't help wondering if he even knew what TV was. And as he sat in the interview chair answering questions about his tribe, it was clear that no one watching would ever know who he really was. And I felt so honored to have crossed ten thousand foot mountains in the rain forest (in the rain) with him. That's who he was.

Brett and Stacy reappeared that day, too. After a laborious retreat from San Locandi, they had recuperated in Punta del Sol, where they'd ended up. They weren't madly in love with us at this point, defending an angry platform that 'they'd been completely abandoned in the middle of the jungle, for no reason at all.' I had little to say, had never disliked them, just saw early on, and pointedly in San Locandi, that they didn't understand the basic tenets of rapid travel by foot. I'm not sure what they thought we were doing out there, but everything they said and did contradicted the natural laws of time and space economy.

Orlando's final responsibilities were to get Stacy, Brett, and me onto our planes, ship the Jeep back to New York, then finally fly himself and family back there, too. There was some fancy footwork in the airport—in fact, I was there three times before actually departing—paying for our expired visas, and rescheduling flights. During this interval, I resolved to send Ernesto my address. Punta del Sol was tiny enough that the postmaster would know Ernesto. I wrote that I missed the jungle, that I was going back to L.A. now, and that he could write to me in Spanish. Not expecting he had a lot to say, I still felt our friendship deserved more than the abruptest farewell. And I closed my note, "with *muchas bananas*."

I tore myself away from Costa Rica, tears streaming down my face as I finally boarded the plane. I didn't want to end the process of changing, from the deepest place in my soul, that had begun in the jungle. But the plane rolled down the runway.

THE END

EPILOGUE

I MANAGED TO HOLD ONTO my new strength and spirit for a number of weeks after returning. I got busy and continued to incorporate what I'd learned wherever I could. I tried not to be cynical about the western world, the endless commodities and consumption, but it was impossible. So I penned a humorous article about American superficiality, had it published, and thus commenced my journalism career. That powerful turning point was a direct result of living closer to the natural order and verifying that nothing about ourselves, our gifts, our yearnings, our hearts, our abilities, is to be wasted or feared. Nothing. Ever. The American lifestyle and spoiled greed are unacceptable in light of natural law and true human potential.

There was one thin, eight-inch piece of string that I found on the ground in Seekwaweeti after everyone had packed up for the day's journey. I had picked it up and put it in my pack—it had value and would come in handy for something. I not only kept it for the rest of the expedition, but to this day as a reminder about having nothing at all but inner strength, faith, the natural world, and a small tribe enduring the elements.

Another lasting effect of the journey was that, after that night when my spinal cord was so cold that I had to climb into the boys' tent, I've never been cold again. Cold has become relative. Being a little chilly is altogether different than spending a day in a cold, surging river followed by a night in a wet sleeping bag. Knowing I'll soon be warm again is not true 'cold.' True cold means 'not gonna get warm'—no sunshine, no blankets, no heater, no one to hold. Not tonight, and not tomorrow.

As for the physical side of returning to California, that was different, too. Striding along Venice boardwalk, I had to stop myself from leaping over park benches. I'd become a leopard and longed to remain one. In fact, I was so resistant to being back, to being a cog in a wheel of a nonsensical machine, that I wore my stained and obliterated T-shirt and pants from Karakima every single day the first ten days back. This was the self I knew, the self I liked and respected, the one that could do anything. (Though nothing physical was required of me now.) When friends asked why I was still wearing the grubby outfit, I explained that I couldn't let go of those powerful days and nights, and wearing the clothes I'd worn for twenty-four days seemed to help. Being fifteen pounds lighter and clear as the Liberty Bell also underscored the fact that, psychically, I just wasn't fully back yet.

And whenever there was a free moment—pumping gas at the station or standing in line at the bank—I'd close my eyes and plunge back into the jungle, submerging instantly and gratefully into those depths again, until I was yanked back to the here and now.

The dreams that had started way back in San Locandi—those wet, jungle-floor, hallucinatory, anguished dreams of horror, struggle, and hopelessness—continued after I was home, every single night, for weeks and weeks and weeks. I'd wake in the blackness, believing I was crawling across masses of huge soaked leaves in torrents of rain—utterly alone, at the mercy of the jungle void. There was no way out, no one to help me, hear me, or find me. In this dream, any expedition glory was non-existent, only gut-wrenching doubt from the pit of my soul.

In retrospect, I wonder if those dreams were the essence, the deepest core, the critical place in one's gut where there's nothing left in the world except yourself and the raw natural world......and you're still alive. That shake-down, having everything removed except for life itself, is where you meet yourself head on. It's the bottom, yet you're still there...almost like a kind of forgiveness and maybe a new start. You're not dying, you're just staring life in the face like a tiger in front of you. That stare was the Expedition's gift to us.

In L.A., those dreams were the very last thread connecting me to those twenty-four days and nights.

Six weeks after the expedition, Orlando and his four prized 'gringos' were given a photo exhibit at the United Nations (including some of my photos!) and a reception by the United Nations Environmental Program (UNEP). I hadn't seen Orlando since leaving Costa Rica. Obviously we'd all readjusted to 'normal life' again, but it was weird. "How are you doing since the expedition?" I asked him.

"I'm still on it," he replied.

A while later at the ceremony, the Director of UNEP asked Orlando what we found in the jungle, expecting to hear anthropological anecdotes, maybe some tiger sightings.

"We found God," said Orlando.

After a while, the embers began to go out, memories of Ernesto included. L.A. reality demanded attention, and nostalgia doesn't fetch much on the open market. Besides, the life I returned to had its merit (food, shelter, people speaking my language, all the powdered milk I wanted). My photos miraculously survived to illustrate our story; and I got letters and phone calls from Tomas, Orlando, Darcy, Carmela, Brett, Stacy, and even Chela.

Two months after returning, I received a letter from Costa Rica with no return address. It didn't look like Carmela's handwriting.

I opened it to unfold a single sheet of lined yellow paper. "Wendy"—it began, and the rest of the page was in small, even, Spanish script. Knowing it was from Ernesto, I skimmed down the page, so pleased to hear from him. Some of it could be deciphered without a Spanish dictionary. I learned that after returning to Punta del Sol, he'd then gone back to San Jose. But we'd already left and it made him sad. He said two other things that reassured me about the expedition... During some of the difficult times, I had turned inward, instead of giving support to the others. Especially toward the end, there were times when I did not rise above my own concerns and felt bad about it. But Ernesto now wrote, "I enjoyed your company on the journey. You were very kind to everyone—for this I can't forget you." He also mentioned his own misgivings about Orlando's eccentricities, something he'd never imparted at the time, probably due to his loyalties and responsibilities as a worker.

Then he signed the letter, "*Te quiero mucho*," and repeated it in English, "I love you."

Now you, too, have survived the Expedition! Thanks for taking a walk on the wild side.

If you enjoyed the adventure, please do some or all of the following:

- Write a review at Amazon (and elsewhere).
- Read my other books.
- Recommend "Expedition Costa Rica" to others.
- Give copies as gifts.
- Review the book at reader websites.
- Ask your library to carry the paperback and ebook.
- Visit 'WendyRaebeck.com' to see what's coming next, sign onto my email list, and leave comments.

Muchas gracias, con muchas bananas!

OTHER BOOKS BY W. M. RAEBECK:

"I Did Inhale — Memoir of a Hippie Chick"

"Some Swamis are Fat"
          (originally under pen-name Ava Greene)

"Nicaragua Journal —
          Back Roads of the Contra War"

ALSO:

- *Short Story Collection*

- *Poetry Collection*

and more to follow…

CPSIA information can be obtained
at www.ICGtesting.com
Printed in the USA
LVHW081547140223
739479LV00016B/1600